RARE BOOK LIBRARIANSHIP

RARE BOOK LIBRARIANSHIP

An Introduction and Guide

*Steven K. Galbraith and
Geoffrey D. Smith*

Foreword by Joel B. Silver

LIBRARIES UNLIMITED

AN IMPRINT OF ABC-CLIO, LLC
Santa Barbara, California • Denver, Colorado • Oxford, England

Library of Congress Cataloging-in-Publication Data

Galbraith, Steven Kenneth.
  Rare book librarianship : an introduction and guide / Steven K. Galbraith and Geoffrey D. Smith.
       pages cm
  Includes bibliographical references and index.
  ISBN 978–1–59158–881–8 (pbk.) — ISBN 978–1–59158–882–5 (e-book)
1. Rare book librarianship. 2. Libraries—Special collections—Rare books. 3. Rare books—Bibliography—Methodology. 4. Rare book libraries—Administration. I. Smith, Geoffrey D. (Geoffrey Dayton), 1948– II. Title.
Z688.R3G35 2012
025.1'9609—dc23   2012012354

ISBN: 978–1–59158–881–8
EISBN: 978–1–59158–882–5

16 15 14 13 12   1 2 3 4 5

This book is also available on the World Wide Web as an eBook.
Visit www.abc-clio.com for details.

Libraries Unlimited
An Imprint of ABC-CLIO, LLC

ABC-CLIO, LLC
130 Cremona Drive, P.O. Box 1911
Santa Barbara, California 93116-1911

This book is printed on acid-free paper ∞

Manufactured in the United States of America

CONTENTS

FOREWORD

It is really all about the books. And the manuscripts. And the photographs, and sheet music, and ephemera, and objects, and everything else that combine to make a rare book and special collections library. Until recently, collecting physical objects was what all libraries routinely did. A library was based on its physical collections, and the librarians assembled and developed those collections, and they also made sure that people were able to use them. The focus in non-special-collections libraries was on information, and the information was found in books. As libraries ran out of space, and as they embraced newer technologies, the provision of information in the form of microfilm and microfiche became standard in research libraries, and many older books and runs of periodicals were made available this way. If, however, a library did not have a requested work in any form, it could and would borrow it, unless the book was rare and therefore not available on interlibrary loan.

What made librarians consider a book to be rare? Sometimes it was the age of the book, or its relatively high financial value. On other occasions a book was designated as rare because it was a limited edition or it was in a special binding, or it was signed by the author or another well-known person. As institutions gathered enough of these rare books, it became clear that they needed to be physically separated from their circulating companions, and that they also needed special care so that they would not be lost or damaged. Special expertise was required as well on the parts of their caretakers, so that the books could be described properly and then made available to inquiring readers in an appropriate and secure environment.

As more special collections departments and libraries opened in American academic institutions, owning rare books and manuscripts became an accepted and necessary activity for many libraries. The books were there to provide information, and they could also be used to show the history of writing and printing, as well as to provide tangible support for the study of how and what our ancestors wrote and read. Special collections librarians were well aware of the importance and high value of their collections, and they worked to build their holdings through purchase and gift, and to make them available to interested and qualified readers who had the need to consult their holdings. Librarians also mounted exhibitions, published catalogs, arranged for talks and conferences, and spent a great deal of time learning about their collections and answering questions related to them.

Over the last half-century, the profession of special collections librarianship in the United States has grown tremendously, as special collections librarians have worked to organize and define themselves as a separate branch of librarianship, distinct from other specialties in its focus on original objects, but similar to other areas of librarianship in its insistence on the highest standards of service and expertise. During this formative period of special collections librarianship, however, the rest of the world of librarianship did not remain static. The tremendous growth of the use of electronic technology in all parts of society, including libraries and librarianship, has transformed libraries irrevocably from reading and reference rooms with supporting collections of books to providers of information in whatever form can best serve users' needs. In the academic world, it is now usually information in electronic form that users are seeking, and a prospective library user might consider that the best outcome to an inquiry is that the necessary information and resources can be provided without any need to visit the library in a physical sense. Users have come to expect, and librarians are striving to provide, as much information as possible in electronic form. Physical books are still being purchased, but more library users are expecting that the books that they want or need to read will be made available to them in free and searchable electronic form, suitable for any electronic devices they may own now or in the future, from cell phone to portable e-reader.

What does this mean for special collections libraries? Most importantly, rare book and special collections librarians inhabit a world of librarianship in which user access to all of a library's collections—the more immediate the access, the better—is paramount. While previous generations of rare book librarians tended to focus on the building of their collections above all else, today it is access to and communication about the collections that occupy a greater portion of librarians' time. Certainly, collection development has not been forgotten, and librarians, even with their often-reduced acquisitions budgets, continue to make significant additions to their collections. But the ease and expectation of swift electronic communication has changed the way rare book librarians now go about their business, and as

Rare Book Librarianship: An Introduction and Guide makes clear, in addition to knowing about rare books in general and their collections in particular, rare book librarians now also need to stay in touch with up-to-date methods of communication, from the construction of attractive websites to participation in social networks.

There is another consequence for rare book librarians of the recent shift in the way libraries go about their business, and this relates not only to communication with library users, but to communication with administrators outside of special collections. Simply put, books of all kinds will likely be less familiar to future generations than they are to many adults today, and this relative lack of familiarity with books will extend to future generations of librarians. Before the widespread personal and commercial use of the Internet, while technology was certainly not ignored in the curricula of schools of library and information science, the majority of courses taken by M.L.S. students revolved in some way around books rather than around other forms of information. Collection development courses focused on the acquisition of physical materials, and most cataloging and reference emphasized work with printed books. While many students took specialized courses on databases or other technology-related areas, the required core curriculum insured that all professional librarians had a common frame of reference grounded in books. Though there is still some exposure to books within the typical mandated curriculum, this is changing rapidly as schools try to catch up to the transformed present-day world of librarianship.

The changing curriculum for librarians means that future non-special-collections librarians will have little exposure in library school to issues relating to physical books in library collections, and this is of great importance to those who work with rare books. Since it is usually a non-special-collections librarian-administrator to whom a special collections librarian reports, future heads and directors of special collections departments will need to be both proactive and articulate in explaining what it is their units do, and why rare book libraries are deserving of continued funding for the acquisition and care of printed books in an era of tightened budgets and electronic information. While relationships between rare book library heads and their supervisors have not always been close or compatible, there was, at least, a common bond of experience based on the provision of information to users in the form of physical books. As library administrators' views of book collections change, as research library "collections" make the shift from physical to electronic form, special collections librarians need to be even more active and assertive than ever before in demonstrating the importance (and irreplaceability) of rare books and manuscripts.

This need for rare book librarians to convince others about the significance of their collections is not new in American libraries. In 1939, in an article on "The Functions of Rare Books" (*College and Research Libraries* 1, December 1939, pp. 97–103), the UCLA librarian, Lawrence Clark Powell, defended the acquisition of rare books by libraries against those in the profession who believed that libraries had no business acquiring rare books, when there were so many other materials and services competing for available funds and staff time. Powell, who until his death in 2001 remained a strong defender of the central and essential role of books in libraries, also took to task dull and lethargic librarians, who, in his mind, were not making the case for the tremendous good that rare books could do:

> Milton observed that books are not dead things. My observation is that often their custodians are. Because of their historical significance, their intrinsic value, their beauty, and sentimental associations, rare books, when intelligently grouped, have power to excite the imagination and stimulate the intellectual curiosity of the student. A rare book collection, no matter how modest, can be made by alert librarians to play an educational role, and to enliven the library, increase its prestige, and to draw alumni and friends. Whereas the rare book collection in a university library is primarily for research, the smaller the institution the more potent can become rare books in directly influencing the students. The collection can be made to work through exhibits and catalogs, and by class consultations involving students, professors, and librarians, and by special courses given by the library staff in bibliography, book arts, etc. (101)

Many more librarians are doing these things today than they were in 1939, and the present book elaborates on Powell's suggestions and provides many more excellent ideas about how librarians can convey to students, faculty, and the general public both the practical use, and also the magic, of the collections that they hold. The professional literature of rare book librarianship has been reluctant to embrace the extrasensory hold on us that books and other objects can have, but it is precisely this quality that draws the public to visit museums, and occasionally, even to browse the exhibitions at rare book libraries. This undeniable attraction, which Lawrence Clark Powell once termed "the alchemy of books," is the rare book librarian's greatest asset, and it can be called upon whenever he or she reaches out to others to share with them the importance of the collection and the joys and rewards that can come from contact with it.

For guidance on the varied attractions of books, today's librarian need look no further than the classic article on book collecting by A. W. Pollard that appeared in the 11th edition of *Encyclopaedia Britannica* (1910–1911). In trying to articulate what draws a collector to a rare book, Pollard wrote that "to attract a collector a book must appeal to his eye, his mind or his imagination, and many famous books appeal to all three." This appeal to the eye, the mind, or the imagination applies no less to library visitors than to book collectors, and librarians can and should take full advantage of the beauty, the importance, and the evocative qualities that their books possess, to entrance visitors, educate students, and satisfy researchers. If librarians are able to do this consistently and successfully, they are well on the way to fulfilling their essential responsibilities as custodians of the world's most important cultural treasures, and this achievement will not go unnoticed by their supervisors, both inside and outside the library.

Joel B. Silver
Bloomington, Indiana

INTRODUCTION: "OUR TIME" AND STAYING RELEVANT

At the 2008 RBMS[1] Preconference held in Los Angeles, UCLA University Librarian Gary Strong opened the meeting with an eloquent welcome that included a phrase that echoed through the rest of the conference: "This is our time." The idea resonated because it was both inspiring and fundamentally correct. Unique or rare items held at libraries should become all the more valuable in an era in which libraries increasingly share resources, both print and electronic. Indeed, the more that libraries develop their collections in relation to other libraries on which they co-depend on resources shared through consortium subscriptions and lending, the more homogeneous library resources become. The exception is the materials held in special collections, which should progressively appear all the more special. The rare and unique holdings of libraries should increasingly define what makes libraries distinctive.

The key word here is "should." The statements above "should" be true. It makes perfect sense to librarians who are in the know. To us it is clearly "our time" (One wonders what profession doesn't believe that it is their time?). But what does the outside world think of the importance of rare books and other special collections material? What does your university administration think? How does your local and state government feel? Most outside the library community might be surprised to learn that it is "our time," because it is doubtful that anyone has actually told them that it is. By the time of the publication of this book, Strong's rallying call of "our time" will be about four years old. Depending on when you are reading this book, it could be much older still. One hopes that during that time, special collections librarians and archivists have been working to prove Strong's point. You can be the judge.

Creating a present and future that is unquestionably "our time" is the challenge of special collections and rare book librarians in the early twenty-first century. Our libraries have the strength of unique and rare primary resources, but that alone is not enough. We must stay relevant and we must do so proactively. We must demystify the frequent perception that the rare book library is an exclusive unit operating autonomously from the larger world of librarianship. We must learn to communicate effectively the importance of our collections at a time when libraries are underfunded and overlooked (and these times occur regularly in the life of a library). Technology is also undoubtedly a crucial part of this challenge. We must keep up with current technology and trends and meet our users where they are, rather than expecting them to come to us via traditional library points of contact such as the reference desk and the online catalog (and both of these need to continue to evolve as well). This, of course, means digitizing our material, not least because these rare materials are physically inaccessible except at our holding libraries. Users have come to expect digital access and this is a positive thing. Providing digital access is a difficult challenge, but a challenge that every librarian needs to embrace.

A HYBRID LIBRARIAN

Meeting the challenges of creating "our time" can only be done when rare book librarians are first successfully engaged with what some might say are the more traditional responsibilities of the profession. The core challenge is to achieve a healthy balance between access and preservation. In other words, how does the librarian meet the needs of library users while also meeting the needs of the artifacts, which are often not in perfect condition and will always be deteriorating at some level? Finding this balance is not new but has always been the challenge of working with rare materials. The nature of this challenge, however, changes from era to era, and from collection to collection.

Meeting the needs of access and preservation relies on fundamental skills that are based in bibliography, that is, the study of books as material objects. Indeed, the most exciting aspect of rare book librarianship is the hands-on work done with historical artifacts. Whether writing up a conservation report, teaching a user how to handle rare materials, digitizing an item, or choosing material for an exhibition, having books in your hands is always the highlight of the job. In order to perform any of these tasks properly, you first need to understand the physical makeup of books and how they were produced. You need to know how to handle a book in a way that causes it the least amount of stress and reduces the risk of damage. You need to know how to evaluate a book's condition and whether it is stable enough to be used or should be conserved or perhaps preserved digitally. To this end, an active conservation and preservation program must be ongoing. Therefore, the librarian needs to be able to work with conservators, which requires a basic knowledge of their terminology and techniques.

Rare book librarians also need to stay ahead of the curve when it comes to the digital world or, at the very least, keep up. In particular, they must keep current with the standards and practices of digital imaging, while also preparing for a future when digital access will be a free service to their user community. They will have to engage with various forms of social media as a means of outreach and access. Librarians will continue to catalog books with traditional controlled vocabulary, but they also need to acknowledge the growing use of social metadata, as libraries use Next Generation online catalogs to invite their community to tag, annotate, and review their items. Social metadata is actually very well suited to special collections, which tend to have a focused user base. Turning to our users to supply metadata for our artifacts makes sense, considering our users are the ones working most closely with them.

Rare book librarians must always be engaged in outreach to their communities, in order to get their materials into the hands of scholars and students, and into classrooms and exhibitions. Far too often librarians buy into the myth of the captive audience. No library—not a university library, not a public library—has a community of users on which they can passively rely. Every library and every division within a library has to engage in outreach and demonstrate their value to their community. This often comes down to meeting your users where they are, rather than taking the more passive "build it and they will come" approach. If you don't reach out to users, they won't come. If you are not actively demonstrating the worth of your resources, you will not even get the support you need to "build it."

Today's rare book librarian is undoubtedly a hybrid librarian with skills rooted in centuries of book production, the latest digital technology, and tools and strategies for outreach. Do not make the mistake of believing that choosing a career in rare books means you will be working with "old books" in splendid isolation. From booksellers to book historians to book conservators, the world of rare books is one actively engaged with technology and the digital world. Similarly, on campus and in local communities, rare book librarians need to be dynamic, visible ambassadors of their collections. This does not mean you have to be some impossible combination of Johann Gutenberg, Steve Jobs, and P. T. Barnum. But it would not hurt.

LIBRARIAN-SCHOLAR

By now a career in the field of rare books may seem overwhelming. Now throw in a second master's degree (a PhD is sometimes preferred), one or two European languages (perhaps in addition to Latin), and the ability to write successful grants and work with donors. This is quite a tall order. But it is all in reach. The field is a demanding one, but that is also the joy of it. To the right person, all the facets of the job should be appealing. Meeting the diverse challenges of rare book librarianship usually leads to continuing your education once you are in the field. Continuing education is crucial for a rare book librarian. Although not stated in job ads, intellectual curiosity and a commitment to lifelong learning are key qualities of a rare book librarian.

Librarianship has a long history of scholarship and is currently producing exciting research, but on the whole it is sometimes not viewed as a particularly scholarly field. Rare book librarianship is a slightly different story. Rare book librarians and curators are often scholars in their own right. In many ways the field demands it. A rare book librarian needs to interact with his or her users not only as a colleague but also as an expert in the field. That expertise comes from hands-on experience, to be sure, but it is sharpened and enhanced by the production of original scholarship. All of those planning on careers in rare book librarianship and those currently in the field should feel encouraged to contribute to the scholarship in areas of librarianship, book history, or in whatever fields their research takes them.

RARE BOOK LIBRARIANSHIP

The aim of this book is to help prepare students for a career in this exciting and challenging field and to offer guidance to librarians who are relatively new to the field. It is a multidimensional profession to be sure, and there is a lot of ground to cover. We focus on what we believe to be the core skills and knowledge needed to successfully manage rare book collections, including suggested practices for: handling, housing, and conserving rare materials; collection development and working with book dealers and auction houses; and user education and outreach.

Many of the topics discussed in this book are applicable to the broader category of special collections. Some may find the decision to write a book focused on rare book librarianship to be strange at a time when most librarians working in special collections are responsible for a mix of different media. This point of view is certainly understandable. But rare book librarianship is a field of specialization and deserves to be treated as such. There has been no recent book focusing on rare book librarianship since Roderick Cave's *Rare Book Librarianship* (London: C. Bingley; Hamden, CT: Linnet Books, 1976; rev. ed. London: C. Bingley, 1982). Cave's book continues to be helpful (portions of it are still used in rare book courses), but it is out-of-date, particularly considering the rise of digital technologies and the growth of the history of the book as an academic discipline. A new book on rare book librarianship has long been needed to reflect advances in the way rare books are studied, handled, housed, and preserved.

We hope this book is a productive combination of the knowledge and experience of two rare book librarians working in two different contexts and specializing in different fields. The first is a seasoned librarian who works at a large public university and specializes in modern American books. The second is a younger librarian who has worked primarily at an independent research library and specializes in early modern European books. Between the two of us we clearly do not cover all the bases, but we hope our experiences help produce a broad view of the field that will be instructive to our readers. We also hope that the examples we share will prove valuable. Rather than simply describe and explain, we try to illuminate key points in this book by sharing real-life examples from our own experiences and from those of our professional colleagues.

We frequently joke that we knew more about rare books ten years ago than we do today. That is to say, having learned the conspicuous fundamentals of rare book librarianship, it is easy to assume naively that you have become a master of the field. We are, however, acutely reminded, year to year, day to day, moment to moment, about the diversity and depth of the field of rare books and how much more there is to learn. We offer this proposition not to be daunting but rather encouraging. Rare book librarianship is a lifelong learning experience that leads to great professional pride and profound personal gratification.

NOTE

1. RBMS stands for the Rare Books and Manuscripts Section of the Association of College and Research Libraries (ACRL). ACRL is a division of the American Library Association (ALA).

CHAPTER 1

A Brief History of Rare Book Libraries

For the purposes of this chapter, the history of rare book libraries concentrates on the relatively recent development in the late nineteenth century and forward of many great library and private collections that would form the cores of the modern rare book libraries housed in research institutions. Still, some brief discussion of early books will demonstrate the evolution of the concept of the rare book library over time.

In the early history of books from the preprint era, most libraries were rare book libraries because books themselves were rare. One need only to read the description of the Clerk in "The Prologue" to Geoffrey Chaucer's *Canterbury Tales* to have a contemporary sense of the value of manuscript books, circa 1400: "For he would rather have at his bed's head/Some twenty books, all bound in black and red,/Of Aristotle and his philosophy/Than rich robes, fiddle, or gay psaltery." With the advent of printing in the West in the mid-fifteenth century, book production did proliferate but not to the extent that books were readily available to the mass population: that would occur after the eighteenth century. The importance and value of early libraries, determined greatly by rarity, is attested to through the inclusion of books as major inherited legacies of family estates. The documentation of books and entire libraries in wills and testaments, alongside property and cash, furniture and animal stock, confirms the value of these volumes for families from the medieval to modern period.

Despite the increased production of books in the early print era, they still remained relatively rare. The larger monastic and university libraries of the sixteenth through eighteenth centuries would typically contain thousands of volumes, and libraries of modestly wealthy individuals would average hundreds of volumes. When, in 1638, the library of John Harvard was bequeathed to the fledgling New College of Cambridge, Massachusetts (thus earning the donor eternal academic recognition), it numbered about 400 titles. Close to 200 years later, Thomas Jefferson's library, accorded to be the largest library in the United States, numbered between nine and ten thousand titles, approximately 6,500 of which would form the core of the Library of Congress, whose earlier holdings had been burned by British troops during the War of 1812.

Within the American context, then, almost all early libraries were, in essence, rare book libraries. The early development of American circulating libraries was almost exclusively through private means with circulation restricted to membership. Benjamin Franklin and friends founded the Library Company of Philadelphia in 1731, and subsequent private libraries—such as the Redwood Library and Athenaeum in Newport, Rhode Island (1747), the Charleston Library Society (1748), the New York Society Library (1754), and the Boston Athenæum (1807), among scores of private libraries across North American population centers—would be founded through the mid-nineteenth century, when the public library movement supplanted these elite institutions, most of which do, however, thrive today. These early private libraries, too, were all rare book libraries, for the collections, predominantly imported from Europe, were of the type that forms the core collections of many academic and public rare book libraries today: pre-1800 literature, history, philosophy, law, medicine, and natural and physical science.

The formation of early private and institutional libraries however, was not so much a conscious effort to collect books as rare books as it was the assembly and preservation of the books of the time, though many of those books would ultimately form the core of several great rare book libraries today. Not to display facetiousness, but rather express a truism, the great rare book collections of Oxford, Cambridge, and the British Museum (now the British Library) exist largely because these institutions were there when the books were first printed. These institutions were also depositories for the Stationers' Company, which regulated British publishing, so that all books published in England would automatically become part of their collections. Isaac Newton's *Philosophiæ Naturalis Principia Mathematica* (1687) resides at Oxford University, for example, because it was deposited there at the time of its printing. Continuing Oxford University as an exemplar of an early deposit library, and to emphasize further the contemporary, quotidian view toward deposit books, Oxford sold its Shakespeare First Folio of 1623, the first collection of his plays, in 1664 because that edition was seemingly superseded by subsequent folio editions in 1632 and 1663. (Oxford reacquired their copy in 1906 when the concept of a rare book had evolved from the seventeenth century.) As late as the nineteenth century, as Edwin Wolf 2nd notes, "the Library of Congress, although it bought Jefferson's library in 1815 to replace its earlier destroyed collection, at first did not consider its books rare books in any sense and saw itself solely as a reference library."[1]

THE GROWTH OF BOOK COLLECTING

When we speak of the history of rare book libraries in the context of the twenty-first century, however, we are thinking in terms of the formal administrative institutions that we recognize today whether they be affiliated with colleges and universities, public libraries, historical societies, or private and special libraries. It is difficult to demarcate exactly when *the* rare book as opposed to a common book became a distinctive concept; indeed, defining rare books today remains variable because books that were previously considered common acquire new significance when new areas of research, such as literacy studies and book history, are practiced by the scholarly community. Further, the development of rare book libraries cannot be viewed in isolation but rather, in the cases of most phenomena, must be perceived as part of a larger, integrated cultural context. Certainly, there have been lovers of books, that is, bibliophiles, since the inception of text, but the formal recognition of a widespread rare book market and the emergence of the genteel book collector can generally be placed in the nineteenth century.

Later in this text, we will discuss the era of modern printing and expound upon the nineteenth century as an era of information explosion, but, generally, the proliferation of cheaper merchandise to vastly expanded markets, all precipitated by the Industrial Revolution, led to a reexamination and recapturing of the cultural estate, at least among the modern, Western nations. At a time when British critics such as John Ruskin and Walter Pater and American critics such as Henry James and Henry Adams were extolling classical art and, at the same time, championing new art, William Morris, in England, and Elbert Hubbard, in the United States, were revivifying the craft of book arts at their respective Kelmscott and Roycroft presses. In America, the nineteenth century was a watershed period for great museum development and expansion, a movement that would continue well into the twentieth century. New York's Metropolitan Museum of Art and Boston's Museum of Fine Arts were both founded in 1870; the Art Institute of Chicago was founded in 1879. At the same time, cognizance of the importance of rare books is exemplified in the founding of elite book collecting clubs: for example, New York's Grolier Club (1884), Cleveland's Rowfant Club (1892), and Chicago's Caxton Club (1895). Indeed, the late nineteenth and early twentieth centuries are generally accorded to be the era of the Golden Age of Book Collecting.

The vogue of rare book collecting and the development of major thematic collections by wealthy individuals are anticipatory of the growth of institutionalized rare book libraries. Although a mélange of factors contributed to the book collecting vogue, three developments were particularly influential.

First and foremost, the collecting market defined high-spot acquisitions, most notably such works as Gutenberg's Bible (c. 1455) or Shakespeare's First Folio. These high spots not only defined great collections but also inflated the values. Books accessible to the modestly wealthy collector from earlier periods became increasingly restricted to the very rich such as J. Pierpont Morgan, Henry E. Huntington, or Henry Folger. Secondly, the classical, medieval, and renaissance revivals of the Victorian era, much in response to the modern industrial era, also revived interest in the acquisition of antiquities, including books. And, thirdly, in academic circles, the concept of the canonical author became codified. Again, using the conspicuous example of Shakespeare, he was always considered a great writer and influence, but in the late-eighteen and nineteenth century the vogue of the Bard and the near deification of Shakespeare elevated his reputation to new heights and, concomitantly, escalated the value of those works published in his lifetime. In the English-speaking world, British writers—Spenser, Milton, the Romantics—would dominate the late-nineteenth-century canon, but American writers—Hawthorne, Melville, Whitman—would emerge in the twentieth century. And, the collectors' canon was not restricted to literary artists as there were cornerstones for all areas of knowledge: for instance, Galileo and Newton in the physical sciences, Galen and Vesalius in the medical sciences, and Aristotle, Aquinas, and Luther in philosophy and theology.

ACADEMIC RARE BOOK LIBRARIES

Academic libraries, in large response to the development of the research university, increasingly recognized the difference between the mass of their general collections and the select volumes of primary and canonical resources that were identified as rare books as we think of them today. William Joyce notes that:

> The rise of the research university and the founding of scholarly organizations created, through peer review and criticism, scholarly standards and professional expertise that extended knowledge in a variety of disciplines ... This process of professionalization in the academic disciplines resulted in the identification and creation of a scholarly canon of significant texts in many fields, but especially in history and literature, where the recently adopted elective system in university curricula created greatly expanded opportunity for research and teaching in these areas.[2]

Of course, libraries have always had a sense of the treasures under their stewardship and the development of actual rare book departments follows a familiar pattern common to most academic libraries: sequestration of identified rarities; assignment of personnel for administration (bibliographic control, cohesive development, stewardship, etc.); and designation of special facilities and storage.

In the United States, as would be expected, the earliest academic rare book libraries, as defined as distinct administrative units, began at elite private institutions whose extensive and long-term holdings included thousands of rare books in need of special security, care, and development. At Harvard University, for example, medieval manuscripts, early printed books, and other rare materials had been part of the library system for a couple of centuries. For instance, after its owner's death in 1817, the library of Christian Daniel Ebeling, "with thousands of American maps and rare newspapers of the eighteenth and early nineteenth centuries, was bought for Harvard college."[3] Harvard had special rarities as well—for instance, John James Audubon's *Birds of America*—that were part of the Harvard library system because Harvard alumni and officers subscribed for an item at its time of publication. Alfred Claghorn Potter in his 1934 *Library of Harvard University* alphabetically lists by subject dozens of special collections, from American history to Yiddish literature, with notations that document the rich tradition of private donation.[4] When Harvard's great Widener Library opened in 1915, a Treasure Room was designated and the aforementioned treasures were thus housed there. Treasures continued to be added to the Harvard collections, such as Amy Lowell's Keats collection in 1925. Recognizing the historical richness and research value of its special holdings, Harvard opened the Houghton Library in 1942, the first academic building dedicated solely to rare books.

Driven by external social and education movements, as enumerated above, Harvard's pattern for the development of rare book collections, as an exemplum, was not unique to that institution. Yale University followed a similar path. Like Harvard, Yale had thousands of manuscripts and early books and other treasures, including the same Audubon edition as Harvard's, for example, that were moved to special shelving in the later nineteenth century. Upon the opening of the Sterling Library in 1931, a Rare Book Room was designated for the special collections. In 1963, Yale opened the Beinecke Library, the world's largest library dedicated to rare books, and, though some collections remained at the Sterling Library, the Beinecke became the central repository for Yale University's book treasures.

An aggressive acquisition plan was an alternative for the development of rare book collections among those institutions without the long history, and alumni constituency, of Harvard, Yale, and other predominantly eastern colleges and universities. The University of Chicago, for instance, though attuned to the growing appreciation for rare book collections, by necessity followed a different path than Harvard and Yale since it was founded in the 1890s and its library collections were a meager inheritance from the old Chicago University that had closed in the 1880s and the collections of the Baptist Union Theological Seminary. The University of Chicago, with the substantial assistance of benefactors such as John D. Rockefeller, Jr., and others, purchased, *en bloc*, the stock of S. Calvary & Company in Berlin, Germany, which brought immediate eminence to its rare book collections. Although the eventual library that came to Chicago fell short of expectations both in quantity and quality, it remains a remarkable acquisition, for the initial expectations were certainly somewhat astronomical. Robert Rosenthal notes in "The Berlin Collection: A History" that

> the manuscripts were relatively small in number but they were the foundation of the University's later collection. Many came from the library of the marquis of Taccone and not from Pope Pius VII's library as touted; the autograph letters of Raphael turned out to be spurious. The Library's collection of incunabula also had its beginning with the Berlin Collection, but the real impact came from books printed during the later Renaissance and into the eighteenth century. In one stroke, as it were, the Library had books on many subjects, some of which were not to become academically favored for decades to come. The history of science and technology is an example. In more traditional subjects such as paleography and classical philology, there was not only an immediate scholarly audience at the founding of the University, but both subjects became deeply rooted in the University and part of the Library's holdings.[5]

Whether through accretion over time, through sudden, massive investment (a method that would be employed by other institutions, as we shall see), or a combination of both, rare book libraries by the mid-twentieth century were a respected and established resource of the modern research library.

INDEPENDENT RARE BOOK LIBRARIES

At the same time that academic institutions were establishing their rare book libraries, the great library collections of the most prominent book collectors, such as the aforementioned Morgan, Huntington, and Folger, were being monumentalized as privately supported eponymous libraries, museums, and institutes within grandiose structures and settings. The Pierpont Morgan Library (today The Morgan Library & Museum) was founded in 1906 in New York City; The Huntington Library, Art Collections, and Botanical Gardens was founded in 1919 in San Marino, California; and the Folger Shakespeare Library was founded in 1932 in Washington, D.C. These magnificent institutions reflect the esteem and honor accorded rare books and epitomize and endorse the concept of special care and attention to textual treasures that so marked library history in the twentieth century.

Selected U.S. Independent Rare Book Libraries with Founding Dates

American Antiquarian Society, Worcester, Massachusetts, 1812

The John Carter Brown Library, Rhode Island, 1846

The Newberry, Chicago, Illinois, 1887

The Pierpont Morgan Library (The Morgan Library & Museum), New York City, 1906

The Huntington Library, Art Collections, and Botanical Gardens, San Marino, California, 1919

Folger Shakespeare Library, Washington, D.C., 1932

The Rosenbach Museum & Library, Philadelphia, Pennsylvania, 1954

Subsequent, then, to the golden age of collecting and the formal establishment of rare book libraries at academic institutions, not to mention the significant collections at large public libraries such as the New York Public Library and the Boston Public Library, many private rare book collections found themselves, more and more, being donated to institutions. Although some collections, at the behest of the owner or the estate, returned to the general marketplace and were dispersed, still others who wished to retain the bibliographic integrity of their collections sought repositories where the materials would be accessible to research scholars and would be preserved in perpetuity. But the major development in rare book libraries was the post–World War II expansion of public universities and the concomitant growth of library resources, and, for our interest, rare book collections.

THE ESTABLISHMENT OF RARE BOOK LIBRARIES

In most cases, the core collections of public university rare book libraries were the result of gifts. Similarly to private institutions, most public universities had collections of worth prior to formal organization of a rare book department, but the eventual commitment of personnel to oversee and develop the collections further attested to the official recognition of the importance of those collections as essential to a modern research library. The further commitment of space and special equipment and needs, such as security systems, further ensconced the rare book library as a permanent feature of the research library administrative structure. The creation of rare book departments was a national movement that grew rapidly during the three decades following World War II. The University of California, Berkeley's Rare Book Collection was founded in 1954 and moved to its Bancroft Library in 1970. The Ohio State University Libraries created its

Rare Book Department in 1962 and moved to a special room in 1968. One of Ohio State's great collections, the Talfourd Lynn Collection, had been donated to the library in 1954, eight years prior to establishment of its Rare Book Department, and, of course, became a cornerstone of the new rare book collection. The Lilly Library at Indiana University was dedicated in 1960 and its collection foundation was built upon the donations of Josiah Kirby Lilly, Jr., who first donated portions of his private library in 1954. The University of Texas had a long history of rare book collecting, as compared to other public American universities, but the founding of the Harry R. Ransom Humanities Research Center in 1957 centralized Texas's rare books and special collections. Strong institutional and private financial commitments resulted in rapid expansion of collections and resources.

Following the establishment of rare book libraries in public institutions, rare book holdings generally, be they at private libraries, large public libraries, or public universities, experienced rapid growth. In particular, most research libraries, recognizing the wealth of materials in their general collections, initiated massive transfer programs to rare books. We have noted that great European libraries and older, private American libraries had established strong rare book collections because, simply, they existed when the books were printed. In the case of American public universities, many were founded as land-grant institutions after the Morrill Act of 1862; their collections were extremely strong in nineteenth- and twentieth-century holdings. But, as nineteenth- and twentieth-century studies became more prominent research areas, these materials assumed greater importance as primary resources. In *Preserving Research Collections: A Collaboration between Librarians and Scholars* (1999), a joint publication of a task force comprised of the Association of Research Libraries, the Modern Language Association, and the American Historical Association (with representation from other scholarly associations), it was noted that "the print resources of the past 150 years constitute a significant portion of the nation's cultural legacy and are crucial to all areas of the humanities especially." Acknowledging the ultimate need for digitization of these materials, the task force also recognized the need to identify and preserve physically the "nearly 80 million books in North American research libraries" in preparation for the digital effort since "carelessness, accidents, the ravages of use, and the vicissitudes of time have jeopardized the documentary heritage."[6] This white paper precipitated a massive transfer of materials from general collections to special collections at college and university libraries across the nation.

As academic research became more diverse and inclusive, libraries established special collections to meet those scholarly needs. Bowling Green State University founded its Browne Popular Culture Library in 1969; the Ohio State University established its Cartoon and Graphic Arts Library (now the Billy Ireland Cartoon Library & Museum) in 1977; and the University of Mississippi established its Blues Archive in 1984. And, across the nation, special collections were established to enhance scholarly studies of disciplines added to the academic curriculum in the later twentieth century such as women's studies, African and African-American studies, East Asian studies, and, film, photography, and media studies.

RARE BOOK LIBRARIES IN THE TWENTY-FIRST CENTURY

At the onset of the twenty-first century, rare book and special collections appear to be essential components of most large libraries, and that status does not appear, at this moment in time, to be abating. The future of rare books, and special collections, moreover, appears bright due to two primary reasons: increased donations and, in a related manner, increased recognition by library administrators that rare book collections add special distinction to a library system and attract the attention of financial supporters. Prior to the establishment of institutional rare book libraries, the dispersal of private libraries was principally through sale on the open market. In the United States, as we have documented, private donation has been a tradition of over a hundred years for some private academic rare book libraries and a over a half-century for most public university rare book libraries. Outreach and donor relations (as we will discuss later in the text) have suffused much of the prominent bibliophilic community so that collectors are now well aware that there are places where their collections will be preserved and developed. Whether through loyalty to an alma mater, or local, regional, or state pride, or recognition and respect for established institutional rare book collections, there exists a great lure among donors to commit their collections to an institution.

With regard to institutional commitment, the mantra of the first decade of the twenty-first century has been a consistent extolling of the importance of special collections to add distinction to individual library collections. In an era of increasing electronic resources, research libraries throughout the country possess many of the same databases and full-text journals (both current and archival) that meet the scholarly and recreational needs of their mass of faculty and students, but, at the same time, add a veneer of sameness to college and university online catalogs. With the inception of statewide and regional consortia, small college libraries have access to many resources that, because of cost, were once the province of large research libraries only. This is not to disparage the expanded access to this universe of knowledge, which has been such a boon to scholarship at all levels. But the sameness of such collections can distract external interest, particularly from potential donors who are typically attracted to and endeared by uniqueness. To that end, special collections departments are critical to the contemporary library in order to continue to engage the support and participation of faculty, students, and donors.

The commitment to special collections is an investment in the preservation of rare and fragile materials that may not be documented or accessible other than through the physical items themselves at a special collections library. Even with the concerted efforts to make all text and images universally accessible (and we emphasize and endorse these efforts as both invaluable and inexorable), the provenance of a particular book, the uniqueness of certain materials such as manuscripts, the quality of an original item such as prints that need to be examined in person, ensure, for the near future at least, support for the acquisition and organization of special collections.

Furthermore, the absolute value of such collections as critical to scholarly research will drive digitization and conservation efforts. For instance, despite the Google Books Library Project not every copy of a particular book is being digitized, and, though scholars will have access to the text of most books, they may well not have access to every variant printing, author's notes, or contemporary commentary that are contained in the millions of books that will not be digitized. And, beyond the commitment of the local institution, national funding agencies, such as the National Endowment for the Humanities and the Council on Library and Information Resources, to name but two, have traditionally supported access to special collections through cataloging, digitization, and conservation grants.

THE IMPORTANCE OF KNOWING THE HISTORY OF RARE BOOK LIBRARIES

The remainder of this book focuses on specific components of rare book librarianship. It is useful to note here, however, the rich and fabled history and tradition of rare book libraries. Even as every book has its own story, so does every rare book library, and, we would suggest, the similarities of individual rare book libraries—their origins and developments; their missions of access, service, and preservation; their goals and visions—far outweigh their dissimilarities, which are principally the content of collections wherein lie their personal stories. Rare book librarianship is an honored profession that contributes not only to the promotion of scholarship for others but to the intellectual growth of the many diverse librarians actively involved in the field.

NOTES

1. Edwin Wolf 2nd, "The Development of Rare Book Collections in the United States," in *Rare Book Collections: Some Theoretical and Practical Suggestions for Use by Libraries and Students*, ed. H. Richard Archer (Chicago: American Library Association, 1965), 13.

2. William Joyce, "The Evolution of the Concept of Special Collections in American Research Libraries," *Rare Books & Manuscripts Librarianship* 3, no. 1 (Spring 1988): 24.

3. Albert Predeek, *A History of Libraries in Great Britain and North America*, trans. Lawrence S. Thompson (Chicago: American Library Association, 1947), 100.

4. Alfred Claghorn Potter, *The Library of Harvard University*, 4th ed. (Cambridge, MA: Harvard University Press, 1934; Boston: Gregg Press, 1972).

5. Robert Rosenthal, "The Berlin Collection: A History," in *The Berlin Collection. Being a History and Exhibition of the Books and Manuscripts Purchased in Berlin in 1891 for the University of Chicago by William Rainey Harper with the Support of Nine Citizens of Chicago* (Chicago, 1979), 1–23. http://dlf.grainger.uiuc.edu/dlfcollectionsregistry/browse/FullDisplay.asp?cid=70207.

6. *Preserving Research Collections: A Collaboration between Librarians and Scholars*, http://www.mla.org/rep_preserving_collections.

FURTHER READINGS

Harris, Michael J. *History of Libraries in the Western World*. Metuchen, NJ: Scarecrow Press, 1995.

Lerner, Fred. *The Story of Libraries: From the Invention of Writing to the Computer Age*. New York: Continuum, 2009.

Wendorf, Richard, ed. *Rare Book and Manuscript Libraries in the Twenty-First Century*. Cambridge, MA: Harvard University Press, 1993.

CHAPTER 2

Rare Books as Texts and Historical Artifacts

PART I. BIBLIOGRAPHY AND BOOKS FROM THE HAND-PRESS PERIOD (1450–1800)

Bibliography, in all its varieties, is the backbone of rare books librarianship, for it is the scientific analysis of all aspects of the physical book and the concomitant placement of a particular artifact in the history of printing. All administrative, professional, public, and social functions associated with rare book librarianship go for naught if exact identification of books and other materials is lacking or incorrect. We would suggest that the greatest joy of any rare book librarian is the actual handling of books for the purpose of description in all its physical aspects, from format to paper to type to binding and more. Too common is the rare book librarian who laments the time required for administrative tasks that detract from the physical engagement with the actual collections.

Bibliography is an academic field of its own and cannot be covered comprehensively in a single rare book librarianship course: deep understanding of the many aspects of the physical book and book culture emerges gradually through years of experience in the field augmented by scholarly study. The literature of bibliography is extensive and even the most experienced bibliographer has recourse to consult outside sources. Book description has been rigorously documented and codified over the centuries and there are standard bibliographic guides and histories that should be part of the personal library of any rare book librarian. Most prominent among the guides to bibliography are: Fredson Bowers, *Principles of Bibliographical Description* (first published in 1949, Oak Knoll Press, 2005); Philip Gaskell,

A New Introduction to Bibliography (first published in 1972; Oak Knoll Press, 2009); and, Ronald McKerrow, *An Introduction to Bibliography for Literary Students* (first published in 1927; Oak Knoll Press 1994). There are many additional, useful bibliographic texts, both broad and specialized, that will serve bibliographers with particular depth in areas of specialization.

TYPES OF BIBLIOGRAPHY

There are several types of bibliography, from the straightforward listing of references to the detailed analytical description of single books. Each branch of bibliography is important and serves a distinct purpose. The most common bibliography is the listing of scholarly references and resources that have been consulted for research publications. Although simple and direct in presentation, these bibliographic lists are indispensible for the promulgation of knowledge as they link other scholars to the expanding universe of a research area. Though description of the materials is typically minimal, it must be emphasized that regardless of the level of analysis, the bibliographic data must be accurate. The annotated bibliography adds substantive content description to the reference list and serves the further function of summarizing and, in some cases, evaluating the works at hand. Whereas reference lists are background to a reasoned and developed thesis, annotated bibliographies are often scholarly works in their own right organized around a particular topic, genre, or author. This does not preclude a reference list from being annotated, but in general practice the extent of an annotated bibliography makes it expensive and impractical to print. In either case, such bibliographies are supplemental or preparatory for other research publications.

More germane to rare book librarianship are analytical and descriptive bibliographies that are self-contained works about specific textual artifacts, and though they may be important for research in other areas, they are at the same time independent research documents. In brief, as propounded by Fredson Bowers, analytical bibliography is the detailed examination of a single physical book. Traditionally, certain components are required for analytical bibliography that will be discussed in more detail below, but include imprint, format, collation, colophon, etc. But a thorough analytical bibliography can be greatly expanded, and for some historical, iconic texts like the 42-line Gutenberg Bible, can be virtually comprehensive in accounting for description and placement of every type mark. In the end, a good, thorough analytical bibliography should unambiguously identify a single book and differentiate it from other seemingly identical copies.

A descriptive bibliography is an amassing and comparison of multiple, individual analytic bibliographies in an attempt to describe what the ideal copy of a printed item would be. That is to say, a descriptive bibliography is a comparative document that is essential in assessing individual copies that may be in one's possession. Although not synonymous, analytical bibliography and descriptive bibliography are integral to each other. In modern study of print history, analytical bibliography is useful for informing reading history, reader response, and literacy studies. A comprehensive analytical bibliography, then, would include such unique information as personal and institutional bookplates, inscriptions and presentations, annotations, and other marks. An analytical bibliography would also include alterations to the book over time: original bindings and subsequent rebinding, text block repairs or alterations. A thorough descriptive bibliography places the text in the broader historical and cultural context. It is derived from the many individual analytical bibliographies, and includes the date and place of printing, text construction as conveyed through the collation, and origin of the type font and paper. In general, the bibliographic data of the descriptive bibliography should apply to all the copies from a press run. If individual copies vary from the ideal description then such changes must be noted.

Analytical and descriptive bibliography, then, are essential for the precise identification of particular texts and placement of those texts in the larger historical and cultural context. Such information is important for two broad reasons: reliable access to the collections and accurate identification of a library's holdings. Visiting scholars and researchers rely upon bibliographic description in the planning and strategy of their academic projects, particularly in cases when scholars travel from great distances to view collections in person. Precise identification of materials also ensures claims to missing items that may, by whatever means, become the property of another individual or institution.

BASIC DESCRIPTIVE BIBLIOGRAPHY

As suggested at the beginning of this chapter, it would take a series of courses and years of experience to truly educate someone in the many areas of bibliography. Creation of physical texts and visual histories has been a mainstay of all civilized cultures from their earliest inceptions, from stone inscriptions to Egyptian papyrus manuscripts to medieval manuscript codices, movable type, machine press and digital books. But there are a few basic areas of descriptive bibliography for printed works that every rare book librarian at the outset of his or her career should be familiar with.

Format

First and foremost is a book's format: the number of times a printed sheet was folded to form its leaves. Typically, for an introductory class, the predominant formats will provide a sound basis for fledgling rare book librarians and include, with their standard abbreviations: folio (2°), quarto

Terminology

In addition to the terms used in analytical and descriptive bibliography explained in this chapter, the rare book librarian needs to know the language used to describe the physical makeup of books. These are the terms used in catalog records, conservation reports, and descriptions of items for sale in bookseller and auction catalogs. Below is a selection of terms that you will encounter most often. For a more comprehensive list, see John Carter and Nicolas Barker's *ABC for Book Collectors*.

Boards: These are what you might already call the covers of the book, though to be more exact, the boards are the protective materials used for the front and back of a bound book. The materials used to make boards range from wood to pressboard/cardboard, which are then typically covered by a binding material.

Edges: There are three outer edges on a text block: the fore-edge (the long edge opposite the spine), head (top) edge, and tail (bottom) edge.

Endpapers or Endleaves/Flyleaf/Pastedown Leaf: These are the leaves inserted by the binder that precede and follow the printed body of text. They are often the blank leaves found at the beginning and end of a book. Endpapers typically contain a pastedown leaf, which is attached to the board. The term *flyleaves* is sometimes used in the general sense for all front and back free endpapers.

Gutter: The center of an opened book, where the two facing pages meet and disappear into the spine.

Head/Tail: The top and bottom of a book.

Hinge: Where the boards connect to the text bock on the inside of the binding.

Joint: Where the boards connect to the text bock on the outside of the binding.

Leaf/Recto/Verso: People often think of pages when they think of the units of paper found in a book. Bibliographers tend to think in leaves. A leaf is a piece of paper containing two pages. The front side of a leaf is the recto side. The back is the verso. Leaves are created when a sheet of paper is folded. A folio (2°), for example, is a sheet folded once, thus creating two leaves or four pages. A quarto (4°) is a sheet folded twice, creating four leaves or eight pages.

Opening: Two pages (verso | recto) facing each other in an open book.

(4°), octavo (8°), and duodecimo (12°).[1] A folio is a single folded sheet (creating two leaves or four pages), a quarto a double folded sheet (creating four leaves or eight pages), and an octavo, commonly a triple folded sheet though there are other configurations (creating eight leaves or 16 pages). Each additional format—duodecimo (twelves), sextodecimo (sixteens), octodecimo (eighteens), etc.—has greater variety of folds and becomes increasingly difficult to identify. In addition to identifying format through the number of times a sheet was folded, there are factors to determining format, which we will get to shortly.

Format must not be confused with the *size* of the book, which is chiefly determined by the size of the printed sheet prior to folding. Sheets of paper came in a variety of sizes from which Gaskell notes three common sizes: pot, demy, and royal (moving from smaller to larger).[2] Thus the dimensions of a book are not indicative of format. For example, a folio from a smaller sheet size may actually be smaller than a quarto from a larger sheet size.

Format, in fact, may be the most apt topic from which to launch a discussion about the rudiments of printing and bookmaking. The fundamentals of printing include the essential materials—paper, type, and ink—and the basic machine for producing early books, the common hand-press (see figure on p. 24). Format and sheet size cannot be understood without a discussion of papermaking, and subsequent identification of chain lines and watermarks for confirmation of format. It is useful to enhance discussion of artifacts with video presentations of actual manufacturing and production processes and, if possible, to schedule a hands-on workshop with a papermaker, type foundry, and/or print shop.[3]

Paper

The earliest media for recording of text and images were stone inscriptions, Egyptian papyrus, and animal skins, principally parchment and vellum. These were used through the Middle Ages and the manuscript age until paper, a significantly cheaper material developed in China, became the primary medium of the print age. All early paper was handmade and is referred to as *laid paper*, the standard for printed books for 300 years. To make laid paper, a papermaker dips a mould into a vat of pulped rags until the mould is about a third full. With the skilled shaking of the mould, the papermaker binds the fibers together then turns the layer, the inchoate paper, into another felt-bottomed mould. Each layer is subsequently pressed to exude as much moisture as possible until the layer can actually be handled, pressed again and hung to dry. The dried paper is next dipped into a sizing solution, which will create an "impermeable" surface and prevent bleeding of the ink. The completed sheets of paper were gathered into "20 quires of 24 or 25 sheets each," a ream of 480 sheets (common in England and Holland) or 500 sheets (common in France and Italy).[4] Laid paper is identified by wire and chain lines, indelible marks left on the paper by the mould. The mould also usually left a watermark, the design of which often distinguished the paper's size or maker.

The direction of the chain lines, vertical or horizontal, and the location of the watermark provide a clear determination of a book's format. With regard to the more common formats, a folio will have vertical chain lines with the watermark in the middle of leaf 1 or leaf 2; a quarto will have horizontal chain lines with the watermark in the middle of the spine fold of leaves 1 and 4 or of leaves 2 and 3; and an octavo will have vertical chain lines and the watermarks, if the octavo has been folded from a whole sheet, will be at the head of the spine fold of leaves 1, 4, 5, and 8, or of leaves 2, 3, 6, and 7, or, if folded from half sheets, at the head of the spine fold of the four leaves, or no mark.[5]

Chain lines and watermarks may not be visible to the naked eye. In order to reveal them a cold light pad may be used. Often the size of a standard sheet of paper, the cold light pad emits light but not heat. When the pad is placed carefully behind a sheet of paper with the ambient light dimmed, the light from the pad should shine through the paper and reveal the chain lines. Watermarks can be a bit trickier. The printed text tends to obscure them. Working with pages with little or no text will make it easier to locate and examine watermarks. Rare book libraries should have a cold light pad or two at the ready for use by staff and researchers. If you are working with a loose sheet of paper, a light table may serve the same purpose.

With each progressively smaller format, beginning with duodecimo, the identification of exact format becomes more difficult because of varying imposition of type on a sheet of long duodecimo (vertical chain lines) as opposed to a sheet of common duodecimo (horizontal chain lines) or a sheet of inverted duodecimo (vertical lines, again). Recourse to outside references, such as McKerrow and Gaskell, is clearly in order, even for the very experienced bibliographer when it comes to smaller formats. Without doubt, the identification of formats is best done with actual books in hand enhanced by full-sheet facsimiles, which should become permanent resources of any rare book librarianship instructor.[6]

Type

The second component of printing is type, which, when inked, impresses letters and symbols upon the paper. Again, as with all components of bibliography, the study of type is a field unto itself. The identification of type design is better deferred to a specialized course, but an understanding of the basic manufacture of movable type and its application in the printing process is essential for rare book librarians. In brief, printing type is a physical replica of a letter of the alphabet or other symbol (number, punctuation mark) in reverse image that, when inked and pressed to paper, leaves an

Placing a cold light pad under a leaf reveals the paper's chain lines and watermark. In this case, vertical chain lines and a watermark in the center verify that this edition of Samuel Daniel's *The Complaint of Rosamond* is a folio. The watermark is a unicorn. (Annie Immediata)

image. Of course, it was the development of movable type, principally by Johann Gutenberg, that changed the world with regard to the proliferation of knowledge and ideas through the efficient production of hundreds of copies of printed books as opposed to single manuscript books. The interesting fact about type manufacture is that the process descends from harder to softer metals until the final medium, ink, results in liquid, albeit of high viscosity: first, a letter was cut into steel; secondly the steel punch was hammered into a copper matrix; next, a molten alloy of lead, tin, and antimony was poured into the matrix and solidified to a single piece of type. Throughout the process from the punch to the matrix to the type, there is much rasping and filing to make the type uniform and smooth. Durable as they were, type did wear out and new type had to be cast from the matrices, which most early printers had on hand. In the sixteenth century, however, type founding developed as a separate trade and printers more and more purchased cast type from these entrepreneurs:

> The cost of the equipment for a fairly small type foundry was about three times the cost of the equipment for a printing house of average size; and printers were chronically short of capital. ... These foundries bought up the best available materials and employed the finest punch-cutters; and by the early seventeenth century a growing majority of printers throughout Europe were buying type ready made, rather than having it cast from their own materials.[7]

There was variance in type sizes during the early hand-press period although the general trend of type manufacture was toward standardization, particularly as particular foundries began to dominate the type market.

A font of type included the lower case and capitals of the alphabet, ligatures, punctuation marks, diacriticals, numbers, and an assortment of symbols. The type was allotted according to frequency of use, e.g., many *e*'s, fewer *p*'s, even fewer *z*'s, and so on. Numerous typefaces emerged through early printing, and Gaskell suggests that "it is not practicable to offer more than a general guide to them."[8] For the purposes of an introductory rare book librarianship course, the discussion can be limited the three major typefaces that have prevailed even to the present time: roman, gothic (or black letter), and italic. In early print history each of the three prominent typefaces vied for dominance and, though all have survived, roman type prevailed as the most common type of Western culture with italic type being principally used for emphasis and gothic used for religious texts in early printing and for an antique appearance in more modern printing. Type fonts were enhanced with Greek, Hebrew, Arabic, and other typefaces that were essential to scholastic and religious texts. The extent of type fonts varied greatly among early printers with large printing firms such as Christopher Plantin having a huge stock that enabled them to take on multiple and complex printing challenges. Most printers, however, were small businessmen with limited resources. Whether large or small, Gaskell points out "no two printers of the hand-press period possessed stocks of exactly similar founts of type and of ornaments; a printer's typographical equipment was unique, and identifiably so."[9]

Ink

Ink, specifically, printer's ink, is the viscous material that adheres to paper and transmits letters and words to the reader's eye. Ink, of course, had always been a liquid medium for the production of manuscripts in the pre-print era. Printer's ink, however, was a thicker, paste-like substance adapted for the high-pressure printing press. Printer's ink varied in its ingredients and quality, but, generally, was made up of linseed oil and lampblack.

THE PRINTING PROCESS

Composition and Imposition

With paper, type, and ink in place, the printer is in position to begin the printing process. The process begins with composition, the planning of the printed text. Working from a copy text, usually in manuscript but also in print for subsequent editions, the compositor decides upon format, which largely determines the amount of paper needed for a project, then casts off an estimate of type distribution, a printer's copy: "To this end the compositor—or sometimes the master or overseer—'cast off' the copy by counting words and by computation according to the sizes of type and page that had been decided upon."[10] As noted above, the amount of type available in any given print shop would largely determine the casting off. From a contemporary perspective, casting off is truly a remarkable feat that required much experience. Even a folio sheet of four pages (page 1 and 4 on one side, 2 and 3 on the other) required almost preternatural estimates of typesetting, an estimate that was only complicated by smaller formats with increasing number of pages per sheet, i.e., quarto, 8 pages; octavo, 16 pages; and duodecimo, 24 pages.

With a printer's copy complete, including special instructions for "layout, italicization, capitalization, etc.," typesetting began.[11] Selecting type from the printer's tray, the compositor added the type to a composing stick. Spacers were used to separate words and, finally, for end-line justification. The type would read left to right for the compositor, but otherwise the "letters were upside down and mirror-fashion."[12] The compositor continued to place type in the stick until it was full, usually three to six lines depending upon the size of type as well as the size of the stick. The set type would be placed in a wooden galley and the next lines of type composed. This process continued until a page-length galley was complete and another page begun. As each page of type was completed, it would be tied off with string and set aside until the required number of pages for a sheet was assembled. The composed pages were then imposed, i.e., arranged in a chase or a forme: as noted, 2 pages for a folio, 4 pages for a quarto, 8 pages for an octavo, etc. Subsequently, the remaining pages to be printed on the opposite side of the sheet would be assembled.[13]

Signatures and Collation

It is important to remember, and cannot be overemphasized, that "books were printed . . . not leaf by leaf but on large sheets of paper with a number of pages on each side, which were later folded up to make groups of leaves."[14] Thus each sheet had to be folded in such a way that its pages were in the right order. Moreover, the printed sheets had to be gathered together in the right order. Compositors, then, added signatures to each sheet to ensure that sheets were folded and assembled properly after the printing was completed. Signatures are the letters found in the bottom corner of the recto page of the first few leaves of a gathering. The most common signatures are the letters of the Latin alphabet, 23 letters, A to Z, omitting I or J, U or V, and W. Thus the first three leaves of a folio in sixes (i.e., three sheets folded once and gathered together) would have the signatures A1, A2, and A3. The fourth, fifth, and sixth leaves might not have printed signatures but are understood to be leaves A4, A5, and A6 (it is unnecessary to sign all the leaves in a gathering). Should the number of signatures exceed the 23-letter alphabet, then the subsequent gatherings would be signed with a double or triple letter, Aa or 2A, Aaa or 3A, etc.

One of the basic skills of a rare book librarian is to collate a book. This is the process through which one counts all the signatures in a book. It is a leaf-by-leaf process that will reveal if any leaves are missing or misbound. Once you have finished your collation you will have a signature statement that accounts for each of the book's sheets. For example, the collation of a "perfect" (or compete) copy of Spenser's 1609 *Faerie Queen* in folio is: A-Y^6, 2A-2H^6, 2I^4. While most of the book is gathered in *sixes* (three folio sheets gathered together), the final gathering required only two sheets,

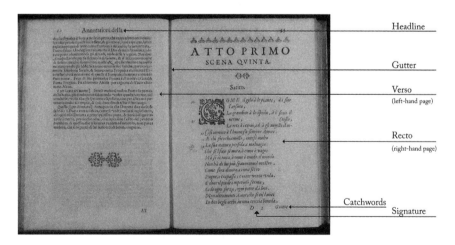

The parts of an open book. (Juliana Culbert)

so it is gathered in *fours*. Comparing your signature statement to one for a "perfect" copy of the same edition will clue you in to any signature variations your book may have.

Catchwords and Preliminaries

As another aid to "help the compositor to get the pages in the right order for printing," a catchword, or the first word of the next page, would be added at the bottom corner of the recto page after the completion of the previous page.[15] Preliminary leaves were typically printed last and included half-title page, title page, prefaces, table of contents, dedications, and preliminary matter; though it should be noted that the title page did not become a bibliographic convention until the sixteenth century. Prior to 1500, printing notes were included in a colophon, or concluding note on the last page of the book, a continuation of the manuscript tradition when a scribe would note the date and place of the completion of his manuscript, often with a clever retort regarding this onerous undertaking.[16] The colophon did not cease with the sixteenth century and was still common into the seventeenth century and continues today with fine press books.

In early printing, the average printer did not own an abundance of type. That is to say, most printers could not afford the luxury of keeping complete formes of set type and, after a print run of a designated number of sheets, the forme was emptied, the type cleaned of ink, and distributed to the printer's tray. In such a manner, as one sheet was being printed, the compositor could simultaneously set type for a subsequent sheet. Rates of composition were measured in "ens." An en is a unit of measurement in typography equal to half the width of an "em," a relative measurement that corresponds to the width and height of the type in the font (that measurement will vary depending on the size of the font). As Gaskell notes, "The number of ens in a setting of type is proportional to the number of pieces of type in it."[17] Some scholars cite a rate of 1,000 ens an hour, though this number may be high. Moreover, so much depends on who was setting the type: some compositors were faster or slower than others. By way of an example, looking at a page from the Shakespeare's First Folio of 1623, one counts 105 ens a line by 66 lines (including headlines) for a rough total of 6,930 ens a page. Using the estimate of 1,000 ens an hour, setting one page of the First Folio took roughly seven hours. This estimate may seem high, but a similar figure is arrived at by Charlton Hinman, who estimates one forme, or two folio pages a day:

> if Jaggard's compositors can fairly be supposed to have averaged anything approaching about 11,000 ens a day, it will be seen that the setting of one Folio forme [i.e., two folio pages] ... would take the compositor about one working day.[18]

Press Work

After the compositor and impositor have completed the typesetting, the printer can begin to print. The printer locks up the pages in two chases, one for the inner forme (type for one side of the sheet) and one for the outer forme (the other side of the sheet):

> The spaces between the type pages and the bars of the chase were filled up with wooden furniture, and long wedges were fitted round the edges. Short wedges, or quoins, were then put in between the long wedges and the inside of the chase, loosely at first so that the string with which the pages were tied up could be unwound and removed, and so that any pieces of type that were sticking up above the rest

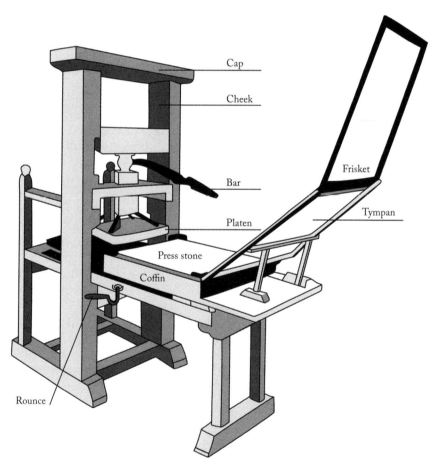

A diagram of an English common press. (Jenna Nichols)

could be knocked down with a wooden planer. Finally, the quoins were driven home with a mallet and "shooting stick" to lock the forme up tightly.[19]

The printer is then ready for the actual presswork. Although there were differences between wooden hand presses, the differences were slight. Wooden hand presses were essentially the same from the earliest printing through the sixteenth, seventeenth, and eighteenth centuries throughout the Western world.

The forme is placed into the bed of the printing press at which time the printer inks it with ink balls, in early printing, and later rollers. Next, the printer attaches a moistened sheet of paper to the tympan, a frame that securely holds the paper so that it will not move during the press run. The tympan is lowered upon the forme, and the forme is moved under the platen, a heavy wooden or metal plate, which is then impressed upon the forme with a pull of the bar by the printer. The result is a printed sheet that is then removed. The sheets are then set aside to await printing on the other side from the second forme. The process continues until the predetermined print run is completed. In early printing the compiled sheets were sold unbound and the purchaser would take them to a bookbinder. Case bindings and trade bindings, standard components of the completed book, would not become standard until the late eighteenth and early nineteenth centuries.

Mere words cannot do justice to the printing process. If possible, a hands-on demonstration at a local print shop is highly recommended for educational purposes.

THE IMPORTANCE OF BIBLIOGRAPHY

Descriptive bibliography, then, records all components of the printing process. In the end, how important is a strong understanding of analytical and descriptive bibliography to rare book librarianship? Many special collections librarians may not even work with rare books but rather archives, photographs, and other visual collections, music, and more. The depth of bibliographic knowledge and experience does, indeed, vary according to the collections under your stewardship. But, certainly, if there are rare books in your collections, it is mandatory to have the preliminary background and to expand on it through hands-on experience and further professional development. In particular, rare book expertise is expected by your library users and those friends and supporters who may someday donate their collections to your institution. They must feel confident in the potential steward of their collections and perceived understanding of how and why books are made is the surest path to a bibliophile's heart. We have spoken about the broad and abstruse academic world of bibliography and we would not think that any

Early Printers

Since the inception of movable type in Europe by Gutenberg in about 1450, many great printers have thrived through the ages. In fact, the study of printing and specific printers is a scholarly area unto itself. It is important that a rare books librarian have a sense of the history of printing, generally, and some knowledge of specific printers. With that in mind we offer a selective list of early printers whose historical prominence and significance are unquestioned.

Johann Gutenberg, ca. 1398–1468: Generally acknowledged as the inventor of movable type in the West. Gutenberg's first large project printing was the 42-line Bible, one of the most famous, and desired, books in the world.

William Caxton, ca. 1415–1492: Caxton, an Englishman who learned the printing trade in Cologne and Bruges, was the first English printer and the first printer of Geoffrey Chaucer's *Canterbury Tales*. Caxton also published many classics and other notable literary works in the vernacular.

Nicolas Jenson, 1420–1480: Born in France, trained in Germany, Jensen later moved to Venice, then the printing capital of the Western world. Jensen is known today for his influential roman type

Anton Koberger, ca. 1440–1513: Koberger established the first printing press in Nuremberg and printed the lavishly illustrated *Liber Chronicarum* (The Nuremberg Chronicle) in 1493.

Johann Froben, ca. 1440–1513: Basel printer who published the works of Erasmus.

Aldus Manutius, 1449–1515: One of the most successful printers in Venice, then the printing capital of Europe, Manutius created italic type and popularized smaller-size books.

Wynkyn de Worde, d. 1534: de Worde was an apprentice to William Caxton and popularized English printed books.

Christopher Plantin, ca. 1520–1589: The Plantin Press of Antwerp, Belgium, was among the greatest of its time. Plantin printed the *Biblia Polyglotta* (Polyglot Bible) between 1568 and 1573.

John Day, ca. 1522–1584: Printer to Queen Elizabeth I, Day was also known for publishing Protestant works, including the monumental *Acts and Monuments* (Book of Martyrs) by John Foxe in 1563 with subsequent editions.

Henri Estienne, 1528–1598: The most famous member of the prestigious Parisian printing family, he directed the publication of the *Thesaurus linguae graecae* (Greek thesaurus) in 1572.

Louis Elzevier, 1540–1617: The founding member of a family firm in the Netherlands, he printed the work of Galileo.

Stephen Daye, ca. 1594–1668: Printer of the Bay Psalm Book (1640), the first book published in Colonial America (the first printing in the Americas dates back to mid-sixteenth-century Mexico City).

Jacob Tonson, 1655–1736: English printer of John Milton, John Dryden, and the first critical edition of Shakespeare's works (ed. Nicholas Rowe 1709).

Benjamin Franklin, 1705–1790: Statesman, inventor, and entrepreneur whose printing business earned him a fortune.

William Strahan, 1715–1785: British publisher, printer to the King, Strahan published Samuel Johnson's *Dictionary* (1755), Edward Gibbons's *The History of the Decline and Fall of the Roman Empire* (1776–1788), and Captain James Cook's *Voyages*.

single rare book librarian would know everything about that vast universe. If we may make an analogy, we do not expect that our family doctor will perform heart surgery, but we certainly expect that he knows the name of our bones, the symptoms of heart illness, or the signs of adult onset diabetes. In our case, we would not anticipate that our patrons expect us to know in depth about Chinese manuscripts from the Ming Dynasty, but we would anticipate that they would expect us to identify and discourse upon a broad swath of book history and book description.

A working knowledge of bibliography is essential for rare book librarians, who need to know how books were produced and constructed in order to study and conserve them. The vocabulary of bibliography is the controlled vocabulary we use when we talk about books with colleagues in our field, whether they be fellow librarians and curators, researchers, conservators, or booksellers.

NOTES

1. Gaskell includes format in his discussion of imposition (the way in which the pages appear on the folded sheet) and emphasizes the most common formats: for, as he notes, "Savage's manual of 1841 illustrated more than 150 impositions" *New Introduction to Bibliography*, 82.
2. For a helpful chart of paper sizes see: Gaskell's *A New Introduction to Bibliography*, 73–75.
3. Filmed at the Plantin-Moretus Museum in Antwerp, *The Making of a Renaissance Book* demonstrates the printing process, from making type to operating the wooden hand

press. This educational video is now distributed through the Rare Book School: http://
www.rarebookschool.org/publications/. The Book Arts Press of the Rare Book School
also has many other useful videos on book production and print history that can greatly
enhance class lectures.

4. Gaskell, *New Introduction*, 59.

5. Ibid., 106.

6. The Book Arts Press is also a good source for full-sheet facsimiles that have been
created for instructional purposes by the Rare Book School.

7. Gaskell, *New Introduction*, 12.

8. Ibid, 16.

9. Ibid., 38.

10. Ibid., 41.

11. Ibid.

12. Ibid., 45.

13. Although much of these sections on composition and imposition are reliant upon
Philip Gaskell's *A New Introduction to Bibliography*, recourse to Ronald B. McKerrow's
An Introduction to Bibliography for Literary Students often provides a clearer explanation of these complex processes. That is to say, both texts should be reviewed in preparation for discussion of composition and imposition. A less detailed but good general
overview of bookmaking is *Esdaile's Manual of Bibliography* (New York: Barnes and
Noble, 1969), a revised edition by Roy Stokes of Aundell Esdaile's work, originally published in 1931.

14. Gaskell, *New Introduction*, 51.

15. Ibid., 53.

16. For instance, a scribe might say "at long last, let's have some wine."

17. Ibid., 54.

18. Charlton Hinman, The Printing and Proof-Reading of the First Folio of Shakespeare (Oxford: Clarendon Press, 1963), 45.

19. Gaskell, *New Introduction*, 79–80.

PART II. MODERN PRINTING

The study of modern printing often receives short shrift in comparison to the
attention paid to early books, particularly fifteenth-century books. Yet,
ironically, American rare book librarians will likely work with more modern
books than early if only because most research libraries developed in the
modern print era. Quite simply, America's great public university systems
originated in the nineteenth century, and especially in the later nineteenth
century under the Land Grant Act, and their collections reflect the later institutional development as compared to some distinguished eastern institutions. This is not to imply that some great early collections have not been
developed (and may yet be developed) at many younger institutions, but
generally, modern collections prevail in terms of both breadth and depth.
Also, as mentioned earlier in this text, rare book or special collections
departments in many public universities are a post–World War II development, decades after the golden age of collecting when many private universities further enriched their early print collections.

Although modern printing is usually designated as beginning at the advent of machine presses in the early nineteenth century, certain conditions, standards, and conventions from the eighteenth century abetted the proliferation of publishing in the succeeding centuries. Particularly in the English-speaking world, the stabilization of the language was a conceptual development that stressed commitment to the national language, and this commitment, in its own right, led to the development of public education and greater literacy. In *The Reading Nation in the Romantic Period*, William St. Clair, an economist by training, examines not only reading, but necessarily, the book and book business. Speaking of the surge of reading in Great Britain in the eighteenth century, St. Clair notes that "by the turn of the nineteenth century, virtually everyone read books, magazines, and newspapers on a regular basis. In the single century Great Britain became a reading nation."[1] During the nineteenth century, the United States would replicate Great Britain's achievement of a century earlier. Notably, the mid-nineteenth century evidences a great expansion of public education in the United States. In 1840, when the United States had 17 million people, there were 47,000 public schools with 1.8 million students. By 1880, the US population was approximately 50 million, close to 3 times the population in 1840, but the number of students in public schools was almost 10 million, 5.5 times the number of public school students in 1840.

At a more abstract level, the English language itself was stabilizing. Observing the change in language from Shakespeare's day, just a hundred years earlier, the Augustans or Neo-Classicists, such as Alexander Pope and John Dryden, recognized the need to standardize the language if the works of the contemporary period were to be still readable in the next hundred or two hundred years. Among associated developments would be a commitment to lexicography and the production of authoritative dictionaries, most notably Samuel Johnson's *Dictionary of the English Language* in 1755 and, in America, Noah Webster's *A Compendious Dictionary of the English Language*, published in 1806, which would proliferate through numerous printings in cheap, popular editions that allowed for autodidacts to learn the meanings of words and rules of grammar, even without attending school. It is a legend among Americans that Abraham Lincoln never went to school, but he likely had a dictionary, a Bible, and access to a cheap edition of Shakespeare. As noted, the concomitant growth of public education greatly increased literacy rates in the Western world. The subsequent craving for texts by the expanded reading public led to new literary forms, alternative print media, and new text dissemination and distribution. Fueled also by the Industrial Revolution, which generated wealth and leisure time, popular entertainment grew and expanded to a wider audience. For the reading public, the growth of the novel, in particular, satisfied a need for entertainment to fill increased leisure time.

The modern age may be best characterized by the emergence of individuality. In terms of printing history this emergence is particularly evident in the development of the independent author, that is, the field of authorship as a distinct profession, one no longer reliant upon patronage. England's 1709 Statute of Anne established the first copyright law and extended legal control of creative works to the individual writer. At the end of the eighteenth century, the United States enacted its Copyright Act of 1790. Though the English, American, and other national copyright laws would expand and alter over the years in order to accommodate new media, the essential intent of such laws remains to guarantee individuals control of their original works. Ultimately, the marketplace became the determiner of new texts: rather than books and other texts coming down from on high, it was the populace who dictated print production, because they were buying the products. That is, they were generating the profits, and the print trade, though many may romanticize it, has always been a business. Gutenberg, after all, developed movable type as a business venture. In the most general of terms, book production went through a great transition, from the printer as individual entrepreneur who controlled the book trade from earliest printing through the eighteenth century, to a separate publishing industry that emerged in the nineteenth century in direct response to a vast new marketplace of readers.

At the advent of the nineteenth century, then, the convergence of steam-powered modern presses, a vastly expanded reading community, and a new model of corporate publishing, largely determined by copyright, led to an explosion in the book market. In comparison to text production during the earlier centuries, the impact of industrial book production during the nineteenth century is analogous to the impact of the information explosion of today's Internet age. As noted, the book trade, by definition, is a business, and the book business of the nineteenth century was exceptional. For instance, in the United States in 1850 there were 673 printing and publishing firms in 25 states. By 1880, there were 3,467 publishing firms in 42 states.[2] In addition to the lower cost of production due to power presses, the book trade was further abetted by cheaper materials, particularly paper (typically the most expensive component of book production) and trade cloth bindings (really casings) as opposed to handcrafted leather bindings. It should be noted that though book production was considerable, the publishing explosion also included newspapers, magazines, almanacs, pamphlets, catalogs, assorted promotional materials, and more. Every aspect of American culture—the arts and entertainment, politics and government, business and industry, high society and low society, science and religion—was promulgated and distributed via a vast print media.

From 1850, the earliest date for which manufacturing census data is reliable, the increase of printed material is clearly documented (and, in a side note, the beginning of reliable manufacturing data in 1850 is a fact that attests to not only increased text production but to the official codification of the information industry). As Scott E. Casper in his introduction to *A History of the Book in America: The Industrial Book, 1840–1880*, notes:

> the number of manufacturing establishments in the US with annual product of at least $500 rose from 153,000 in 1850 to the 254,000 in 1880, a 66 percent increase, while the workers in those establishments nearly tripled. . . . Printing and publishing accounted for a rising share of the manufacturing economy. The number of those establishments multiplied more than fivefold, from 673 in 1850 (0.5 percent of the total manufacturing economy) to 3,467 in 1880 (1.37 percent of the total manufacturing economy), and their employees more than sevenfold, from 8,268 (0.86 percent of all manufacturing workers) to 58,478 (2.14 percent of all manufacturing workers).[3]

These figures represent the printing industry only. But, the universe of text production also includes "bookbinding and papermaking, engraving and lithography, the production of ink, type and printing equipment and the stationery trade."[4] When these industries are integrated, then, text production accounted for more than 4 percent of America's manufacturing laborers and more than 3.5 percent of its total manufactured products.

Hellmut Lehmann-Haupt remarks "there can be no doubt that in the three centuries between 1500 and 1800 not nearly as many technical changes took place as in the decades between 1800 and 1890."[5] It is not within the purview of this text to describe in detail the rapid technological changes in the printing and publishing industry (Lehmann-Haupt notes the registration in the year 1904 of "the 1520th patent for a composing machine" alone, among the multiple technological innovations to the printing processes, such as papermaking, binding, printing presses.)[6] Rather, attention will be given to broad areas of new technology that most influenced the proliferation of print materials from the nineteenth century forward, for "there is no invention in the field of printing and bookmaking which is not the result of a keenly felt need, which is not based on an already existing process and which in turn does not cause and make necessary further new inventions."[7]

Movable type, which opened the print age in the mid-fifteenth century in the West and changed book production forever, prevailed for about 350 years until stereotype plates would initiate a series of new processes for industrial printing. It should be noted that handset type by small presses would continue to exist and does so to this day among fine presses, but stereotype plates, developed in the mid-eighteenth century and introduced in the United States in the early nineteenth century, would dramatically increase the speed of print production. A stereotype plate is a facsimile of a handset forme of movable type created by taking a papier-mâché cast of the forme that was then used as a mold from which metal printing plates were cast. As Philip Gaskell notes, "stereotype plates, normally mounted and imposed as separate pages, were printed exactly like ordinary typeset pages, and it is usually difficult to tell whether a particular book has been printed from type or plates."[8] Easily stored, stereotype plates were perfect for large press runs and subsequent printings that met the nineteenth-century reading public's growing demand for texts. Plates were also easy to reproduce and transport so that standard popular works could be readily reprinted at diverse geographical locations. Furthermore:

> The process also came to be of fundamental importance in the printing of periodicals. By the mid 1830s *The penny magazine* reached the unprecedented sale of 200,000 copies in weekly and monthly parts, which could scarcely have been produced from type alone. Stereo rotaries printed the major newspapers from the mid-1860s, when it also became common for flat column-stereos to be sent from London to the offices of provincial journals, so that local papers would include both typeset news of local origin and syndicated matter in plates from the capital.[9]

Stereotype plates would be used throughout the machine press period with, as with any basic product, technological improvement.

Electrotype plates were developed in the 1840s and eventually became more popular than stereotype plates. To create an electrotype plate, a wax mold of a forme of type was made and coated with graphite so that it would conduct electricity. It was then bathed in copper sulfate alongside a copper plate. An electric current caused copper particles to travel from the plate to the mold until it was coated with a layer of copper. Strengthened and attached to a printing plate, this copper layer became the printing surface. As Gaskell notes, even though "the process was slower and more expensive than stereotyping ... the copper surface of an electro was harder than stereo metal, and the plates were more durable."[10] Plate technology was adaptable to and concomitant with the development of steam-powered machine presses, such as cylinder presses, which could print both sides of a sheet in succession and rotary presses, which utilized curved stereo plates.

Invented in 1886 by Ottmar Mergenthaler, the Linotype typesetting machine further facilitated increased print production particularly for newspapers. Rather than having to set individual pieces of type by hand, the Linotype machine allowed typesetters to produce an entire line of type mechanically by entering text via a keyboard. As the typesetter typed, corresponding matrices for the letters were arranged in a line, creating a mold for casting one line of text. Hot metal in the machine then poured into the matrices producing one complete line of type. The Linotype machine greatly increased the speed of production and made it possible for a small number of pressmen to generate type for many pages of text per day. The Monotype machine worked in a similar, though more complicated fashion, producing a ready-to-print galley of individual pieces of type rather than one connected line, which made for easier typographic corrections.

Improvements in print production, in terms of quantity, continued to occur through the nineteenth and twentieth centuries. Among the vast number of innovations and adaptations in the print industry, two general areas deserve special mention: photographic technology and lithography. Early photographic books "contained actual photographs mounted on the pages," but it was the introduction of photogravure by Karl Klič of Vienna in 1879 that revolutionized photographic reproduction. The image of a photograph was etched directly "on to a copper plate which was grained with resin dust for the reproduction of tone."[11] The development of a rotary press for gravure printing further improved photographic reproduction: "rotogravure, as the fully developed process was called, was established in 1890–95, and was used for the reproduction of the highest class of book and magazine illustrations during the rest of the machine-press period."[12]

Developed by Alois Senefelder in 1798, lithography is a technique based on the chemical repellence of oil and water. An illustration is drawn onto a flat stone with a grease pencil, while the rest of the stone is coated with water. When ink is applied to the stone, it is repelled by the water and accepted by the grease drawing. Thus when placed in a printing press, the illustration is the only part of the stone that is printed. Lithography "was the first fundamentally new printing technology since the invention of relief printing in the fifteenth century."[13] Lithography was particularly important for it expanded the use of color illustrations and adapted well to photographic reproduction. Illustrated books, of course, have existed from the earliest years of the print age. The woodblock illustrations from the *Nuremberg Chronicle* (1493) or Andreas Vesalius's *De humani corporis fabrica* (*On the Workings of the Human Body*) and engraved illustrations from Audubon's *Birds of America* or the steel engraved illustrations in the 1911 edition of the *Encyclopedia Britannica* are among the many iconic illustrated books. Illustrations not only elucidate scientific, technical, and historical matter but also stand as individual art objects. The mid-nineteenth century saw the rise of illustrated magazines, particularly, in England, the *London Illustrated News* (1842) and in America, *Harper's Weekly* (1857). Lithography, and later, photolithography, met the profound popular demand for both weekly newspapers (hundreds of thousands of subscribers for each) and the resulting profits, not only from subscriptions but also advertising, incited a major growth industry of illustrated materials.

At the same time that improved and efficient means of production were being established in the nineteenth century, papermaking kept pace to supply the public demand for print media. Paper (or papyrus or parchment or vellum) has always been the most costly component of any individual book, but with the advent of mechanized papermaking in the late eighteenth and early nineteenth centuries, books and other printed media became less expensive to manufacture and more people could afford cheaper editions of literary classics, popular literature, scientific journals, and other sources of entertainment, instruction and enlightenment. Traditionally made of rag, the inception of wood pulp paper (aided in no small measure by the vast forests of North America and mechanized forestry) reduced significantly the manufacturing costs of printed material. Gaskell notes that "in 1800 all paper was made, rather expensively, by hand; in 1900 more than 99 per cent of it was machine-made," and, though we today lament the acidic, poor-quality paper period of the nineteenth and twentieth centuries, the contemporary public welcomed the vast production of books and other printed material that were disseminated throughout the literate world.[14]

The final component of book manufacturing that resulted in the model of the book as we view it today was the development of cloth case bindings in the early nineteenth century. Though not part of the actual printing process, case bindings replaced the traditional process of storing printed sheets for individual binding in leather or paper and, thus, "immediately offered economies of scale, and combined with the technique of prefabricated casing to lower the unit price of binding, so that it became cheaper to bind a large than a small fraction of an edition at a time."[15] Cheaper binding methods would continue to be incorporated into book publishing, and nineteenth- and twentieth-century readers would have access to cheaper and cheaper books from dime novels and reprints of classic works, often in colorful wrappers, to the ubiquitous paperback editions of today.

The prototypes of modern printing developed largely in the nineteenth century would prevail into twentieth century with continued innovations such as phototypesetting, which resulted in greater efficiencies and lower costs of production, only to be superseded by electronic and digital text production. Modern printing and affiliated media (e.g., lithograph, chromo-lithography, photography), then, has resulted in a wealth of varying materials of great research value. Before discussing the substantive nature of modern materials, it must be noted that modern printing and associated forms of reproduction present challenges and rewards in compiling collections of nonbook materials. Whereas early collections are almost exclusively focused on the codex or book format, modern collections include broadsides, pamphlets, illustrations, photographs, film, music, computer graphic arts, and more. This is not to say that nonbook, or ephemeral, formats did not exist in earlier times—proclamations nailed to public buildings, for instance—but time itself eroded much of the documentation that was destined for obsolescence. Simply by being temporally closer to the nineteenth and twentieth centuries, in addition to the greater mass of ephemera produced, there is a greater chance for the preservation of materials. Moreover, in the modern era, when millions of literate people have the will and the means to save documents other than books, the sheer mass of documents ensures a higher preservation rate: homes with attics, basements, closets; garages and barns; old trunks. Ephemera was preserved by individuals, organizations and corporations. Photographs were saved in specially designed albums; scrapbooks are warehouses of ticket stubs and theatre programs; other personal items, such as postcards or menus were saved for nostalgic value. The public library system itself made provision for preservation of newspapers and magazines. Private companies maintained business records including advertising materials and trade catalogs.

At this point, in a slight digression, we must emphasize that the works of the great writers, historians, philosophers, and scientists, what we might call the classics, will always be cherished, collected, and preserved in rare book libraries. Yet the classics became so because they survived in the libraries of the noble and wealthy classes whereas the reading matter of the common classes were more vulnerable to the ravages of time. Certainly, Shakespeare, for instance, gives us views of common people—Nick Bottom, the weaver from *A Midsummer Night's Dream*—but usually in a comic fashion (Nick Bottom, through a fairy spell, does turn into a donkey, after all) since Shakespeare's attention is focused on the nobility. Would it not be astounding, then, if a work by Nick Bottom existed and we could perceive the Renaissance age from the perspective of a weaver? Such is the case with many materials from the nineteenth and twentieth centuries when novels and memoirs of the working class, immigrants, and minorities have survived and proven to be outstanding research resources.

The publishing explosion of the nineteenth and twentieth centuries, especially in its variety of types of publications and the diverse audience that read these works, opens up great opportunities for research libraries to develop major collections of great scholarly worth. There are those collections developed by individuals with a clear focus on unorthodox or atypical, noncanonical topics that may actually precede scholarly interest, or more colloquially, be ahead of the academic curve. Oftentimes these forward-thinking, nonacademic collectors have passed on and deposited their collections before the wave of scholarly interest arrives. These are the types of collections that, due to a lower status on the institutional priority list, may languish with minimal catalog records only. Collections focused on local history, commercial topics, or popular culture, for instance, often found their way to institutional collections only to be heralded as world-class research collections when discovered by the scholarly community at a later date. Collections that may have been academically déclassé a half century ago are lauded today as invaluable research collections for the study of history and culture and include such areas as jazz, blues, and other popular music; comic books and comic art; children's literature; cookbooks; records of social activism (civil rights, labor, student movements); and trade catalogs.

Virtually every major research library can document the donation of large, nontraditional modern collections that, unlike the canonical collections, can be greatly expanded upon at much lesser expense. The individual items in these collections may not have great value though each collection will undoubtedly have some jewels. It is the proverbial case of the whole being greater than its parts, for it is the intellectual focus and breadth of these collections that provide the depth of research value. With such collections in hand, they can often be augmented by transferring holdings from general collections which are replete with nineteenth- and twentieth-century titles at many libraries.

The Ohio State University was the fortunate recipient of the Emanuel Rudolph Collection of Children's Science Books. Emanuel Rudolph was a former Chair of Botany at Ohio State with a specialty in lichens: his research took him frequently to Antarctica, and there is an Antarctic lichen named after him. In addition to being a great scholar, he was an inveterate book collector. He collected in many areas, but one area of great interest to him was children's science. Upon Professor Rudolph's untimely death in 1992, that collection came to Ohio State. It numbered over 8,000 titles. Upon receipt of the collection, it was evaluated by an external and objective specialist in the field who simply said: "You have a world class collection." Comprised of primarily American and British publications of the nineteenth and early twentieth centuries (though there are some earlier books and some international books), the Rudolph Collection is, indeed, a research collection that traverses many academic areas. It is useful for the study of early childhood education and pedagogy generally; literacy; history of science, of course; and the book arts, particularly illustration and trade book binding. The Rudolph Collections contains works that Samuel Morse, Alexander Graham Bell, Thomas Edison, and Henry Ford might well have read as children.

Another example of a modern collection of great research value is the Ivan S. Gilbert Trade Catalog Collection donated to Ohio State by a local medical doctor who amassed the collection over decades. As background, generally, trade catalogs are a marketing device to promote products and services. The Gilbert Trade Catalog Collection is comprised mostly of industrial and wholesale catalogs, though there are also abundant retail catalogs. Trade catalogs are distinctive for their predetermined rarity (they were throwaways), and, perhaps most importantly for a research library's mission, their vast amount of data and information about the products of every aspect of life and culture: agriculture, medicine, athletics, beauty products, iron and steel products, hardware, music, and books, virtually every mercantile endeavor. In an era without expansive electronic media, the trade catalog was a direct marketing tool that pervaded all strata of the social structure. (Trade catalogs still have a permanent, though diminished presence today.) As the primary marketing device for American business they utilized the latest in modern printing techniques and innovations. These catalogs were, after all, designed to capture the eye of the customer, be the customer an individual, a small business, or a corporation, so the visual element of a trade catalog is critical to its success. Lithography allowed for detailed illustrations and the further development of chromolithography allowed for production of colored catalogs by the 1850s. By the late nineteenth century photographic reproduction added detailed, realistic depiction of products.

Trade catalogs fall into the category of ephemera and, by nature, are rare, due most simply to attrition. For instance, one of the difficulties in providing bibliographic description of trade catalogs is the frequent lack of copyright or other date. Lack of dating is quite understandable in light of the fact that most of these catalogs were annual, semi-annual or quarterly publications distributed to current or potential customers who, quite likely, would dispose of older catalogs as newer catalogs came in. Such clients did not need dates: if they received a catalog in, say 1908, they knew it was 1908. Some 100 years later, we have lost the contemporaneousness of 1908 and have to scrutinize the trade catalog for styles, models, and other historical evidence to confirm the date of distribution. And, due to the ephemeral quality of trade catalogs, any large collection will contain not just rare, but unique items. This discussion of dating is to emphasize not only the ephemeral nature of these documents, but also, and causally, the intrinsic importance of those surviving trade catalogs for reflection and commentary upon the times.

ARTISTS' BOOKS AND FINE PRINTING

As great a contribution to knowledge and documentation that the publishing explosion of the modern press era incited, it was greatly predicated on improved efficiencies and, significantly, cheaper materials. Despite the democratization of the printing industry wherein cheap editions of the Bible, Shakespeare, paperback novels, and popular weekly magazines became available to a vast reading public, some reacted against the poor quality of mass-produced merchandise such as books, but also including furniture, housewares, fabrics, and more. In particular, William Morris, English artist and writer, launched the Arts and Crafts movement, which resuscitated and advanced traditional craftsmanship using quality materials. Morris's Kelmscott Press became a model for the revival of fine printing and was emulated internationally, the Roycroft Press in East Aurora, New York, being a good example. A late nineteenth-century phenomenon, the appreciation and production of fine press books continues to this day.

Artists' books, (books as art objects), and fine press books typically find their way to rare book libraries. Fine press books are almost always printed in small numbers, even one-of-a-kind books in some cases, and, thus, have preordained rarity. In *ABC for Book Collectors*, Carter and Barker class such books as private press books and notes: "as generally understood, the term *private press* would be applied only to a shop where the work was hand-set and hand-printed. Its editions are likely to be limited in number."[16] Collecting private press books is a conundrum for the very reasons explicit in the definition of such works. Because private press books are most commonly comprised of quality materials, particularly fine paper and design bindings, and because the craftwork of their making is labor intensive, they tend to be expensive. A rare book librarian can be challenged to justify a significant financial outlay for an art object when the library's constituency is more concerned with items of substantive research value. Still, the number of private presses abounds, and the rare book librarian will receive brochures or personal visits from book artists eager to sell their product. And, in fact, fine press books can be a welcome addition to many libraries. First, there is a constituency of book lovers who do, indeed, study books as art objects. Second, for the purposes of instruction, fine press books can provide good illustrations of handmade paper, unique type fonts, and fine bindings. Third, many fine press books commission original texts from prominent writers.

As in the discussion of collection development elsewhere in this text, it is a sound idea for the rare book librarian to have a special collection policy in hand for fine press books. Again, current collections, constituency needs, and donor relations will be influential in establishing any such policy for fine press items. For instance, if the rare book library is a repository of a prominent writer's literary archive, small press publications of the writings of that author could prove useful. Among the innumerable small presses throughout the world, it may be practical to establish a collection of a single press such as Aryan Press or the Gehenna Press to note just two prominent book makers in the small press world. So, too, one could choose to develop a historical collection of former presses such as the aforementioned Kelmscott or Roycroft Press.

THE IMPORTANCE OF MODERN PRINTING

Though modern printing is defined by its technology, from steam-powered presses to computer-generated texts, for the rare book librarian the products of these innovations are of equal import. The variety of outputs can only be touched upon, but the cumulative mass of documentation in all areas of knowledge has resulted in a profound record of modern humankind whose history and culture will be preserved in rare book libraries throughout the world.

NOTES

1. William St. Clair, *The Reading Nation in the Romantic Period* (Cambridge, UK: Cambridge University Press, 2004), 13.

2. Data for nineteenth-century book production cited from Scott E. Casper, "Introduction," in *A History of the Book in America*, vol. 3: *The Industrial Book, 1840–1880* (Chapel Hill: University of North Carolina Press; published in association with the American Antiquarian Society, 2007), 1–39.

3. Ibid., 7.

4. Ibid.

5. Hellmut Lehmann-Haupt, *The Book in America: A History of the Making and Selling of Books in the United States* (New York: R. R. Bowker, 1952), 146.

6. Ibid., 153.

7. Ibid., 147.

8. Philip Gaskell, *A New Introduction to Bibliography* (New Castle, DE, and Winchester: Oak Knoll Press and St. Paul's Bibliographies, 2009), 204. The literature on the history and development of stereotype and, later, electrolyte plates is extensive. A useful resource is The *Lucile* Project, created by Sid Huttner at the University of Iowa and accessible at http://sdrc.lib.uiowa.edu/lucile/index.html.

9. Gaskell, *New Introduction*, 205.

10. Ibid.

11. Ibid., 270.

12. Ibid.

13. For a detailed description of the lithographic process, see "Color Printing in the Nineteenth Century: Lithography" the University of Delaware's website: http://www.lib.udel.edu/ud/spec/exhibits/color/lithogr.htm.

14. Gaskell, 228.

15. Ibid., 231.

16. John Carter and Nicolas Barker. *ABC for Book Collectors*. New Castle, DE: Oak Knoll Press; London: British Library, 2004. Available online at www.ilab.org/download.php?object=documentation&id=29

FURTHER READINGS

Bowers, Fredson. *Principles of Bibliographical Description*. Winchester and New Castle, DE: St Paul's Bibliographies and Oak Knoll Press, 2005.

Carter, John, and Nicolas Barker. *ABC for Book Collectors*. New Castle, DE: Oak Knoll Press; London: British Library, 2004. Available online at: www.ilab.org/download.php?object=documentation&id=29.

Gaskell, Philip. *A New Introduction to Bibliography* Winchester, UK: St. Paul's Bibliographies; New Castle, DE: Oak Knoll Press, 2009.

Glaister, Geoffrey Ashall. *Encyclopedia of the Book*. New Castle, DE: Oak Knoll Press, 1996.

McKerrow, Ronald. *An Introduction to Bibliography for Literary Students*. Winchester, UK: St. Paul's Bibliographies; New Castle, DE: Oak Knoll Press, 1994.

CHAPTER 3

Getting to Know Your Collections

Books as independent entities are the traditional hallmarks of all libraries. Great books will always be great books whose influence on audiences documents the transfer of knowledge, evolution of ideas, and generations of new thought. Beyond the physical book itself, however, is the history of each individual book's ownership and readership, that is to say, provenance. Identifying the history of ownership of books in a rare book collection (or any collection) can enrich the research value of important books and add significance to common books. Within the last three decades, greater attention has been paid to once marginal research areas such as book and printing history, the history of readership, and literacy studies and has incited an increase in interest in the provenance of books.

PRESENTATION AND ASSOCIATION COPIES

In the collecting market, presentation and association copies influence monetary value. Presentation copies are copies of a book that were presented from one person (sometimes the author or editor) to another. An association copy is a book that was once owned by someone associated with the book, such as the author or editor. The term has expanded to include books owned by notable persons. For research libraries additional evidence of the importance of ownership must be adduced in order to demonstrate the added research value of one copy of a book over another one with no provenance information. Most rare book librarians, who are acquiring for a research community and not a private collection, are not necessarily swayed to buy a presentation copy that is merely a signed copy by an author who has no personal connection with the owner. A presentation copy owned by an individual of scholarly interest might be attractive if only to confirm that someone such as Samuel Pepys or Thomas Jefferson or F. Scott Fitzgerald had owned the book, but usually the rare book librarian is more impressed by a book with a formidable association and evidence of use.

For instance, it is obvious that Herman Melville's marked copy of Nathaniel Hawthorne's *Mosses from Old Manse*, at Harvard University's Houghton Library, is of inestimable research value on a multitude of levels. First, in 1850, four years after publication, Melville wrote a review of *Mosses* that was published in two parts of the distinguished journal *Literary World*. Secondly, that review was concurrent with Melville's first meeting and artistic infatuation with Hawthorne in the Berkshire Mountains during the summer of 1850. And, thirdly, Melville was, at that time, working on his own little piece, *Moby-Dick*.

In the Rare Books and Manuscripts Library of The Ohio State University Libraries there is a third printing of T. S. Eliot's *The Waste Land*, a nice copy that because of its condition might sell for around $100. But, again, the association makes this somewhat common, though hardly insignificant book an object of research interest. The owner was Francis Lee Utley (1907–1974), Professor of English and Folklore at Ohio State. Utley was a major influence in the development of folklore as an academic discipline and served as president of the American Folklore Society from 1951 to 1952. One of Utley's primary areas of interest was flood narratives and, in light of Eliot's section on "Death by Water," the commentary of the then Harvard graduate student can be enlightening. But, further, Utley's notes also include his undergraduate lecture notes from Harvard on *The Waste Land* by his teacher and mentor, the legendary George Lyman Kittredge.

In 2003 the Folger Shakespeare Library held an exhibition titled "Thys Boke Is Myne," taken from the very words inscribed in a schoolbook copy of Cicero (1502) by a young King Henry VIII, when he was simply "Prynce Henry."[1] Other books on display that winter included those owned and used by the likes of John Donne, George Eliot, Walt Whitman, and Langston Hughes. The exhibition answered the question, "What can association copies teach us?" with the following:

> Studying the evidence of provenance allows us to assess the size and contents of particular libraries, and compare them with others of the same period. It builds upon our understanding of the patterns of literacy and book ownership, and permits us to speculate on the importance of books in a given society. Insight into the scope and nature of private collections yields information on the history of the book trade and the degree to which men and women participated. Provenance also tells us something about reading habits, tastes, and secular interests as well as connecting us to the lives of historical figures.[2]

Not every book will have such conspicuous associations as the examples cited above but may still provide cultural and societal documentation even if the annotators and commentators remain anonymous. In fact, recognizable books with known associations are more likely to be retained by collectors and ultimately make their way to research libraries. Books of a more ephemeral nature—primers, pamphlets, proclamations, etc.—were not intended for posterity and not designed for durability, dual factors that contribute to a high rate of attrition. Books of church sermons, for instance, were meant to be read and reread to the point of destruction and, hence, went into multiple printings. The book collection of James Stevens-Cox that now resides at The Ohio State University, for instance, included a Church of England *Visitation Articles*, a book "issued to churchwardens and other parish officials [with] a list of questions about the religious practices and moral behaviours of the clergy and parishioners."[3] The copy offers singular insight into church practices as demonstrated in manuscript instructions that accentuate ecclesiastical concerns for a particular place at a given time. "This copy was issued to the churchwardens of St. Stephen's Church at Charlton Musgrove, near Wincanton, Somerset and has three further instructions added in manuscript on the final blank." As the bookseller Maggs' description notes[4]:

> You must followe the directio[n] of ye [the] 119 can[on]. Co[n]cerning this book of articles. / You must followe the direction of ye [the] 87 can [on]. & bringe a terrier [i.e., register of property] therof w[i]th you to the visitation in parchment. / Childre[n] that can saye there catachisme must in the morning at ye [the] visitation be brought to my Lor[d].

Just as Fredson Bowers derided the concept of "degressive bibliography" wherein some books are less worthy of full physical description than others, we should equally deride the concept of "degressive provenance" wherein the record of ownership of some books, including commentary and annotations, is less important than other books. Prescient, indeed, would be the rare books librarian who could predict the new areas of research fifty years hence, and to ignore a book in hand because its cultural importance at a given point in time seems insignificant is a presumption and a heresy.

PROVENANCE

A priority of any rare book library, then, is the recording of book provenance, especially in light of the new areas of academic research described above. Because contemporary rare book librarians are cognizant of these research developments, new acquisitions receive, or should receive, provenance documentation upon receipt. Yet, most rare book libraries have innumerable early acquisitions or gifts that have not been examined for ownership—a retrospective undertaking of supreme importance. In some cases, rare book librarians may be examining books that were added to the library decades ago which, precluding extensive record keeping of acquisitions from the paper file era, will be a burdensome though rewarding and frequently enlightening task.

As noted, it is more effective to trace provenance upon arrival of new acquisitions because, simply, the rare book librarian is closer in time to active records of the book's history. So, too, book dealers will have available their source for the book and perhaps history beyond that immediate transaction. In the case of acquisition of individual libraries, there is, first, the collector who assembled the library and who, as with many assiduous collectors, may have additional provenance notes among his or her documentation. In any case, especially in the age of the electronic catalog, the source of new acquisitions should be added in a "note" field of the catalog record. In the instance of gifts, either individual items or entire libraries, a gift note should be noted, if only as a starting place for further provenance research.

Researching a Book's Provenance

Whether the books are newly added to or long existent in the library collection, provenance research begins with a physical examination of the book for signs of ownership. The most common evidence is, of course, the owner's signature, a mark of ownership that has existed from the beginning of books. Although there is no guarantee that the signature is that of the actual previous owners, one is inclined to believe so with obvious exceptions. As an extreme example, should the signature "William Shakespeare" appear in a library copy of the revised second edition of *Holinshed's Chronicles* (1587), the source edition for *Macbeth* and other history plays, one would be more than duly suspicious of the authenticity of this signature, in addition to others such as Jonathan Swift or Gilbert du Motier, Marquis de Lafayette or Jack Kerouac. Fortunately, the legitimacy of such iconic names is usually easy to verify or discredit. The point is, however, that most signatures in books are genuine and, though perhaps not as iconic as those mentioned above, might still be the names of historical personages of some importance.

Such signatures, in period handwriting, are often accompanied by additional information, such as: date and place of purchase, gift of, presented to, etc. In other cases, there may be a series of signatures, especially in books handed down through family and friends. Early books and libraries were, indeed, valuable commodities that often stayed in families for generations. If signatures can be ascertained, then further investigation may yield more facts about the owner and descendents particularly if they are of some prominence and appear in public records. Of special importance are probate records that frequently record the dispensation of books and libraries.

With bibliographic comparison (as will be discussed below), a 1587 *Holin-shed's Chronicles* may be traced to its original owner, if not Shakespeare, and, even if provenance information may still have gaps and can demonstrate only what happened to the book from, say, 1815 until the library acquired it, still a significant historical linkage will have been established.

Akin to signatures and with the same challenges of verification and research are bookplates and book labels, which are nearly as old as printed books themselves.[5] Bookplates and book labels are differentiated in that the former are usually larger or more ornate than the latter, which tend to provide only the owner's name. Bookplates often record the name, coat-of-arms, and motto of the owner. The literature on the history for bookplates is extensive and again, for established figures, easy to verify, though, as always, caveat emptor with regard to forgeries. Even if the bookplate is real, however, that does not guarantee that it was originally affixed to the book in hand. For instance, a bookplate of Charles Dickens in a copy of Wilkie Collins's *The Woman in White* (1859) would be a grand association copy, but, although the bookplate might be genuine and the book itself a first edition, the bookplate could have come from another source and been added to book years after Dickens's death. Still, as with signatures, bookplates are a beginning point and may lead to startling revelations.

Beyond direct evidence of ownership as documented in signatures and bookplates, books should be examined for other marks such as annotations, commentary, deletions, and corrections. Though such markings may not provide further indications of ownership, they are a historical record as to how the book was received and read through the ages. It is especially informing to researchers when varying hands from different eras are manifest in the book.

After all, external evidence, i.e., information added subsequent to the printing of a book, should be examined bibliographically. An accurate analysis of a book is critical to confirm its identity in earlier bibliographies and catalogs, particularly if external evidence is lacking. There is no guarantee that an exact match of a book in hand can be made with its earlier historical existence, but there is a possibility, especially with the accretion of copy-specific information. Libraries of esteemed individuals often have detailed catalogs. Auction records and book dealer catalogs are other helpful resources (and a surprising number turn up on Google Books). Even if a positive match cannot be made, comparisons may indicate that a book in a contemporary library could not possibly be the same copy from the library of the Earl of Ashburnham, for example. Though a disappointment, negative comparisons at least limit possibilities, and the provenance search can go on.

Obviously, few rare book libraries have the resources to conduct such thorough provenance research as described above. Such records do exist for the world's most famous books, such as Gutenberg's 42-line Bible or

Shakespeare's First Folio, whose provenance in some cases is complete from original to contemporary owner. But, the information gleaned from a hands-on examination by someone trained in bibliography will provide the basis for further research by different hands. With the current research focus on the history of the book and print history, it may well be the research scholars who use the rare book library who will complete the provenance search should they have a reason to consult the book in the first place, perhaps lured by a catalog record or bibliographic entry that notes "with the signature and commentary of John Montagu, 4th Earl of Sandwich," or "with the bookplate of Richard Brinsley Sheridan."

As you do acquire more information on the history of a book, start a curatorial file for that book. Such a file could begin with your own acquisition records (the most current provenance information) and should also contain conservation treatment reports (if applicable), and reference questions and scholarly work pertaining to the book. If you see a copy of the same edition of a book in your collection for sale, you may want to add a photocopy of the bookseller's description to your book's curatorial files, being sure to mark clearly that the description is *not* of your copy, so it is obvious to your colleagues and future rare books librarians. If it is a description written by one of the more established booksellers or auction houses, it should provide valuable information on the book. At the very least it provides a current value, whether in the form of a price or auction estimate. As we will now discuss, assessing the value of books is sometimes a part of a rare book librarian's job, and having current prices at your disposal is a great help.

ASSESSING THE VALUE OF YOUR BOOKS

Appraisal Requests

From time to time, rare book librarians should expect a query from someone from the general public who wants to know the value of a book he or she owns. Family bibles are the usual suspects. If your library is known for specializing in a certain subject or author you should expect the occasional request for appraisals along those lines. As you can imagine, the Folger Shakespeare Library gets its fair share of queries regarding the value of Shakespeare editions (usually from the nineteenth century).

To avoid any conflicts of interest, rare book librarians need to be clear that they are not in the business of appraising books. To prepare for such queries, maintain a list of local appraisers. You may want to create a space on your website (perhaps on the FAQs) that explains your library's policy on appraisals and provides links to resources such as the membership directory of the Antiquarian Booksellers' Association of America (http://www.abaa.org). You may also want to link to a helpful page created by the Rare Books and Manuscripts Section (RBMS) of the Association of

College and Research Libraries (ACRL) called "Your Old Books" (http://www.rbms.info/yob.shtml). Here your patrons will find the answers to most of their questions regarding their old books. You could also point them to bookseller sites such as Alibris (alibris.com), ABE.com, Biblio.com, and viaLibri (vialibri.net), which allow users to search the inventory of thousands of booksellers simultaneously. They might be able to find a match for their edition and its current market value.

While guiding your patron to an appropriate appraiser or to resources that would help them to research the book's value on their own, an effective librarian needs to show respect and interest in their book. Always treat the person on the other end of an email or phone call as if he or she were a potential friend of your library. Who knows what other books the person may own or what they might consider donating to the library in the future. Be courteous and helpful, and the good will you show may have rewards down the line.

Appraising Your Own Materials

While rare book librarians can happily pass when asked to appraise family bibles, there will be at least two occasions when you will have to research the value of books. The first is for checking up on a book's price before buying it. The second is for assigning insurance values for general insurance needs and for exhibition loans. Appraising the value of books can be difficult, but fortunately there are helpful resources to assist you.

Reference Books

There are several reference series that record the prices of books sold at auction or through booksellers. *American Book Prices Current* or *ABPC* (New York: Bancroft-Parkman) records the prices of books and other artifacts sold at auction in North America and the United Kingdom, as well as various auction houses throughout Europe. This reference series has been in print since 1895 and is now available as an online subscription resource. Compared to *ABPC*, *Bookman's Price Index* or *BPI* (Detroit: Gale Research) is a relatively new series, since it began in 1964. While *ABPC* covers books sold at auction, *BPI* indexes the prices of books offered in the catalogs of book dealers in the United States, Canada, and the British Isles. Together these two resources help cover the most recent activities of the book trade, while recording the history of the trade in a way that facilitates searching the provenance of specific copies of books or the history of a particular book in the book market. Both resources have cumulative indexes to help with historical research.

Online Tools

If you prefer online searching, you can bypass printed indexes and directly search the past auctions of individual auction houses. The websites of major auction houses include searchable archives. While the odds of finding a particular book may well diminish when you are searching only a few auction houses, when you do find what you what you're looking for, you not only get the hammer price (which sometimes includes the buyer's premium, an added charge assessed to the buyer based on a percentage of the price), you often get a photo of the item and the description that was included in the catalog. Lot searches are sometimes buried on auction websites, so here are the direct links:

Bloomsbury Auctions: http://www.bloomsburyauctions.com/
(see search box in the lower left hand corner of the page)
Bonhams: http://www.bonhams.com/auctions/ (choose the "Past" tab and search)
Christie's: http://www.christies.com/LotFinder/advanced_search.aspx
Sotheby's: http://www.sothebys.com/ (under "Auctions" choose "Sold Lot Archive")

As mentioned above, searching the current stock of booksellers online has become quite easy with sites like Alibris, the American Book Exchange, Biblio.com, and viaLibri. This is sometimes a very effective way of finding a current price for an insurance value or to check to see if a book dealer is offering you a fair price on a book. The results can be surprising. Quoted a price on an English imprint from the early sixteenth century that one of this book's authors thought was too high, he checked the title on ABE.com. To his surprise he found the same book being sold by another book dealer at a price that he thought was much closer to the book's value. The odds of this happening were quite low, but searching the title in ABE.com took less than a minute.

Catalogs

One of the most effective ways to stay current with the rare books market is to regularly read bookseller and auction catalogs. Beyond being an essential duty for collection development, for most librarians it is also a most enjoyable and informative pastime. Time does not allow us to read through as many catalogs as we would like, but choose selected book dealers and auction houses that have strong offerings in your areas of collection development and make reading their catalogs a part of your regular workflow. As Roderick Cave wrote,

A subscription to the sale catalogues of the principal auction houses, and to the priced lists of buyers at sales, is essential for all but the smallest special collections, and the librarian's duties include the pleasant responsibility of scanning these regularly for material of interest which is coming up for sale.[6]

Insurance Values

Assigning insurance values is a trickier business than simply checking on the current value. Not only do you have to assign a fair value for a book, there are additional, hidden costs that you must estimate, the most important of which is the cost of replacing the book, should one come up for sale or auction. Buying a book at auction, for example, adds a significant amount to the overall cost. There is often a buyer's premium, which can be as high as 25 percent of the price of the book, depending on the location of the sale. Another 10 percent of the hammer price might go to the bidding agent if you are using one, on top of which you'll have to pay to have the item shipped to you. If a replacement is found and purchased, the item needs to be accessioned, cataloged, and housed. Thus you must estimate the cost of processing the book and any materials needed to rehouse the book if needed. Then there is the question of rarity and uniqueness. If an item is unlikely to come up for sale any time soon the insurance value needs to increase. You can get a sense of how often a book has come up for sale by searching the cumulative indexes of *American Book Prices Current* and *Bookman's Price Index*. If the item is unique, then the insurance value certainly must increase significantly.

THE IMPORTANCE OF GETTING TO KNOW YOUR COLLECTIONS

Provenance research and appraisals are both exercises in determining the value of books in your library. The idea of value can clearly mean different things. It could simply refer to the current monetary value of a book. It might speak to the book's research value. Then again, value could also mean the personal value that one might put on a book. Indeed there is something profound in the strong relationships that are forged between readers and their books.

There is also importance in the process of determining the value of books. Appraising your books or researching their histories demands that you spend time studying your books. Moreover, these activities demand that you maintain and organize records concerning your books. In this way, you develop a more detailed knowledge of your collection. You will identify potential exhibition topics and research projects. Getting to know your books on that level will sharpen your bibliographic and research skills, while making you a better advocate for your collection.

NOTES

1. For an online version of the exhibition, including an image of Henry's Cicero, see: Folger Shakespeare Library, "Thys Boke Is Myne," http://www.folger.edu/html/exhibitions/thys_boke/boke.asp.

2. "Markings: Signs of Ownership and Association," Folger Shakespeare Library, "Thys Boke Is Myne," March 10, 2003, http://www.folger.edu/html/exhibitions/thys_boke/markings.asp.

3. Maggs Bros, *STC & Wing: Books Printed in England 1500–1700 from the Library of James Stevens-Cox (1910–1997)* (London: Maggs Bros., 2003), 4.

4. Ibid.

5. See, Brian North Lee, *Early Printed Book Labels: A Catalogue of Dated Personal Labels and Gift Labels Printed in Britain to the Year 1760* (Pinner, England: Private Libraries Association, 1976).

6. Roderick Cave, *Rare Book Librarianship* (London: C. Bingley; Hamden, CT: Linnet Books, 1976; rev. ed. London: C. Bingley, 1982), 36.

FURTHER READINGS

Books on the Move: Tracking Copies through Collections and the Book Trade. Ed. Robin Myers, Michael Harris, and Giles Mandelbrote. New Castle, DE: Oak Knoll Press, 2007.

Other People's Books: Association Copies and the Stories They Tell. Introduction by G. Thomas Tanselle. Chicago: The Caxton Club, 2011.

Pearson, David. *Provenance Research in Book History: A Handbook.* London: British Library & Oak Knoll Press, 1998.

Roger E. Stoddard. *A Library-Keeper's Business.* New Castle, DE: Oak Knoll Press, 2002.

CHAPTER 4

Caring For and Preserving Rare Books

The most important skill that a rare book librarian needs to develop is the ability to handle books carefully. Developing "soft hands," to appropriate hockey slang,[1] is necessary for the preservation of rare material and necessary for the education of others. The dexterity with which you handle a rare book is regularly on display, though you might not be aware of it. Whether you are cradling a book for a user, conducting a workshop, or handling materials in front of your colleagues, your skills serve as a model for others. Librarians, curators, and conservators always need to demonstrate best practices.

The following information on how to handle rare books properly is presented for future rare book librarians and for those currently working in the field, but can also be adopted into instructions for your users, presented as a handout, video, or oral presentation.

TAI CHI AND HANDLING BOOKS

Running the risk of sounding a little flaky, handling rare books is akin to practicing the Chinese martial art of tai chi. Like each motion of a tai chi form, each action you take with a rare book should be done slowly and thoughtfully. Most of us have been interacting with books since we were children. Comfortable with their form, we interact with books casually, and at times even roughly. When handling rare books, we draw upon our personal experience with how a book operates, but we need to block this experience to some degree and approach each book anew. Gaining the ability to slow down your pace and think about each move you make dramatically improves the way in which you handle materials. Turning a page, for example, should be a thoughtful action. Pause. Examine the page for any tears or areas of weakness. Choose a strong portion of the page to hold and then turn the page. You might also pick up the habit of examining each opening for interesting elements such as manuscript annotations or debris, even if looking for such elements is not your principal reason for using the book.

Deliberately slowing down also helps prevent mistakes that come from being too experienced with books. As we grow accustomed to handling rare books, a level of familiarity can sometimes lead to bad habits. A careless casualness creeps in. How can you avoid developing bad habits? When readers mishandle rare material, we know it is our duty to stop and correct them, but when we notice our colleagues doing the same we may hesitate, fearing that we might insult them and ultimately foster bad relationships. Yet, we do need to remind one another.

You and your colleagues should agree that in the interest of the collection it is necessary to point out any careless behavior. Foster an open environment in which everyone feels thick-skinned enough to take another's suggestion. For example, both of the book's authors personally have encouraged our colleagues in our conservation departments to point out any inappropriate handling on our parts. When we are corrected, we thank them. It is not easy to have your own mistakes pointed out to you, but if you can develop candid relationships, the reward is much greater than any temporary embarrassment. Conscious efforts to handle books correctly at all times will lead to positive, habitual behavior. Holding regular staff workshops on handling books is a great way to remind experienced colleagues and train new employees. It also keeps the conversation fresh and provides the opportunity for your colleagues to express concerns and answer questions.

Hygiene for Book Handling

The following discussion of hygiene is not meant to give you any complexes or heighten any preexisting obsessive-compulsive behavior (which is not unknown to librarians). The fact of the matter is that a librarian's personal hygiene affects the health of the books under his or her care. The simplest step a rare book librarian can take to handle books safely is to wash his or her hands throughout the day. This will prevent the transfer of any dirt you bring with you onto the books under your care. Likewise, you need to be aware of how dirty your hands can get working with rare materials. For example, if you are working with a book in leather binding that is producing acidic leather dust, commonly called "red rot," set the book into a cradle and then wash the red rot off your hands before further handling the book. This will avoid transferring the red rot from your hands onto the book's pages. When you are finished with the book, wash your hands again to prevent transferring the red rot onto other books that you may subsequently handle.

While washing your hands after you have eaten and washing off red rot are fairly obvious steps to take, you also need to be aware of other substances that you put on your hands that could be dangerous to rare books. One that might surprise you is hand lotion. Avoid using hand lotion if you plan to handle rare books. No matter how well you rub it into your skin, you will transfer oil in the lotion onto the books you are using. Over time, those oils could reveal themselves in the form of dark stains. Rare book librarians should also keep their fingernails trimmed or be very careful when handling books. Leather bindings, both old and new, are prone to cuts and scratches. Most experienced librarians can attest to how easy it is for a clumsy fingernail to leave a mark on a binding.

TAKING BOOKS OFF OF THE SHELF

Taking a book off of a shelf is one of those seemingly mundane tasks that we have all been doing since we were children. Perhaps it may seem strange to discuss it. Yet major damage can be inflicted on a book if removed from a shelf improperly. Never pull a book by the headcap or top of the spine. Think of how many books you have seen where spine is bent or torn at the top. This damage is caused little by little by all the fingers that have pulled on the top of the spine in order to tip and remove the book from the shelf. If you have never noticed, have a look at the books in your library's circulating stack or even in your own home. This bit of damage may seem minor, more cosmetic than critical, but it is the first step to further and greater damage. Not only does such damage lead to further injury to the spine, but it also begins to split the joints that hold the boards onto the spine and text block.

To safely remove a book from its shelf, hold it firmly by its sides and gently pull it. If you are unable to grasp the book's sides because of the books on either side of it, gently push in those two books a half an inch or so to expose enough of the book to take hold of and carefully remove it from the shelf.

Now that you have removed your book from the shelf, you must decide what to do with the space left in its place. The most common practice is to shift all of the remaining books to fill in the space. If you do shift the books, avoid sliding them all at once. Pick each book up one at a time and move them into place. The act of sliding books across a shelf can cause damage to the bottom of the book's spine and boards (and whatever binding might be covering them), and inflicts unnecessary stress on the book's joints and hinges. The damage may not be obvious but the effects of decades of sliding will eventually be revealed. As always, taking preventative measures now will save on the need for conservation later.

You can avoid shifting the books altogether by replacing the book you've just removed with a shelving spacer. At the Folger Shakespeare Library, books are often replaced with a piece of corrugated cardboard folded twice into a Z-shape, which gives it a spring-like flexibility. The spacer expands to fill the space left by the book. Not only does using a spacer eliminate the need to shift any books, an added benefit is that the Z-shaped fold of the spacer creates a space into which the book's call slip can be placed.[2]

Other things to consider when taking a book off its shelf will probably be more obvious. For example, never reach above your head to retrieve a book. Doing so makes it very difficult to handle the book carefully and increases the potential for various calamities. Always use a stepstool or ladder to bring yourself to the height of the book. Large books that are shelved horizontally should be housed on lower shelves. To remove these books in the most careful manner, use a book truck and transfer the book from the shelf to the nearest level of the truck.

TRANSPORTING BOOKS

All the advice above concerning the handling of rare books really boils down to the notion that the less you physically handle a book, the less risk there is for damaging that book. With this in mind, one last piece of advice: when moving books, use a book cart whenever possible. Most rare book librarians will use a book cart when moving large, heavy books, or multiple books. It is an obvious procedure. But a less obvious procedure is to use a cart to move a small stack of quartos or one folio. It may take a little extra time, but it greatly reduces the chance of an accident and sets a good example for your colleagues.

TO WEAR GLOVES OR NOT TO WEAR GLOVES?

Whether on the job or even at social engagements, rare book librarians and curators should expect to be frequently asked, "Do you wear white gloves when you read the old books?" Those who ask the question are probably unaware of the great, long-running debate in the library community over using gloves or not. It is safe to say that the current standard practice is not to use gloves when handling rare books and manuscripts, the idea being that wearing gloves actually increases the potential for damage. Anyone who has ever worn cotton archival gloves can attest to the ways in which they reduce your sense of touch and inhibit your dexterity. Moreover, most cotton gloves are sewn together in a manner that produces cloth bulges at the ends of the fingers, making the handling of pages even more awkward. Sometimes the bulges can unexpectedly catch a leaf.

A helpful article by Cathleen A. Baker and Randy Silverman titled "Misperceptions about White Gloves" puts the gloves debate into perspective and, in the minds of some, to rest.[3] Not only do they review the ways in which gloves make handling rare materials very clumsy, they examine the question of whether or not handling books with bare hands is even all that damaging. For example, they note that "sweat itself is a slightly acidic liquid composed almost exclusively of water (99.0–99.5%)" and that "given the widespread belief that routine handling of paper with bare hands chemically damages it, it is telling that our research uncovered no scientific evidence supporting this notion."[4] Moreover, they remind us of the number of bare hands that have touched early books, from those involved in making the paper, to the workers in the printing house, to centuries of book owners. "Yet, while these practices occurred extensively in all parts of the world over many hundreds of years, little evidence exists that repeated contact with human skin appreciably deteriorated historic paper."[5] If contact with human skin is doing little damage and gloves increase the chances of damage, then clean, dry hands is the best way to go. If gloves must be worn (particularly in cases where one needs to protect their hands, for example when dealing with mold), Baker and Silverman recommend a "close-fitting, unpowdered, vinyl glove to avoid problems with latex allergies."[6]

NB: Wearing gloves is recommended, however, when working with rare materials such as photographs and three-dimensional objects.

ASSESSING A BOOK'S CONDITION

Assessing the condition of a book is a routine exercise in the life of a rare book librarian and one of the more enjoyable parts of the job. Whether it is examining new acquisitions, preparing conservation reports, or deciding whether a book is in good enough condition to be handled by a library user, rare book librarians need to know how to assess the condition of books effectively. The following are recommended steps.

Examining the Binding (If There Is a Binding)

Begin with the front and back boards. The most common damage found on a book is a loose or detached front board. This is mostly due to the front board doing its job as the protective covering of the book. The more a book is opened, the more stress is put on the joint holding the front board to the spine. Rare book librarians will likely encounter hundreds or thousands of books with the front and/or back boards detached. Most of the time, board reattachment might have to wait, as conservators turn their attention to books with more serious damage. In the meantime, it is best to house books with boards off in a manner that stabilizes them, such as in a phase box. Phase boxes and other housing options are discussed later in this chapter.

Whether leather, paper, or vellum, the coverings used for bindings often show signs of the use they've received over the years. In some cases the scratches and brushes on a binding are merely cosmetic, but in other cases the damage can be so bad that continued use will cause further deterioration. If a binding is unstable, then it might need to be rehoused until a conservator can refurbish it (see "The Top Five Most Common Book Conservation Treatments" below).

Continue assessing the binding by examining the front and back joints, i.e., the outside junctions of the boards and the spine. The tops and bottoms of the joints are where stress often causes them to begin to split. If you find that they are splitting, you want to avoid putting any unnecessary stress on the joints. So do not open the book to an angle greater than 90 degrees. After examining the joints, turn to the inside of the boards and examine the hinges, or the inside junction of the boards and the spine. Be sure that that binding and boards are attached securely.

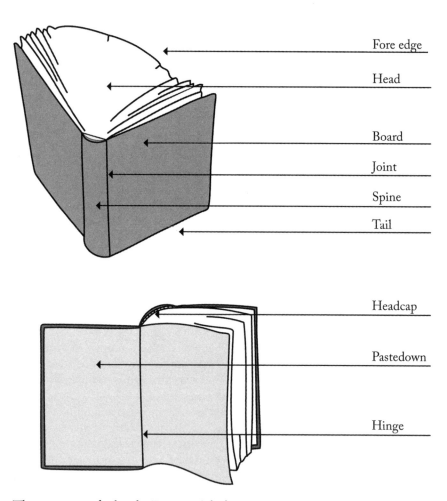

The anatomy of a book. (Jenna Nichols)

Examining the Spine

Common damage to a book's spine includes loose or detached headcaps (from not taking it off of the shelf properly) and damage to the binding on the spine. If the spine appears to be unstable, you'll want to open the book very carefully and gauge whether or not the damage has affected the text block and therefore prevents the book from being opened safely. Most often the damage you see will be superficial and will have no bearing on the text block. Occasionally, however, you'll encounter a book with a cracked spine. Sometimes evidence of a cracked spine will be obvious. You'll notice a crack or cracks that extend through the binding and into the text block. Sometimes the cracks are so major that the text block is broken into several bound pieces. Be careful. A cracked spine may also be simply indicated by a fold in the binding that looks like nothing more than a harmless crease. If there is any evidence of damage to the spine, open the book very cautiously. If you notice major cracks, you may not want to open the book at all.

Examining the Fore-Edge of the Text block

The last step before examining the inside of the book is to take note of the edges of the text block. If there are any signs of damage or fragility on the edges of the book's leaves, you'll need to take special care when turning them. Otherwise you might worsen tears or break off brittle pieces of paper. Also, keep an eye out for any leaves that appear to be sticking out of the text block. These leaves might be loose or detached, or tipped in improperly (see "The Top Five Most Common Book Conservation Treatments," below).

Opening the Book, or, Listening to the Book

Place the book unopened on a book cradle. Often made of foam, book cradles are angled wedges designed to hold books in a way that causes them as little amount of stress as possible. Although some librarians are comfortable with books being opened quite flat, it is best to open books at angles close to 90 degrees, if possible. This will help diminish any unnecessary stress on the book. Once the book is in the cradle, open it from somewhere in the center, paying close attention to the stress you feel from the binding. We might call this "listening to the book." If you are paying attention to the book, it will tell you when it cannot be opened any further. You'll know this when the book begins to tense up and pull itself back closed. Don't open it any further than this angle, if you don't have to. If this opening is smaller than the angle of the book cradle, use additional pieces of foam to build your cradle to the angle that suits your book. If your book opens comfortably to the angle of the foam then all is well, though make sure that being open to that angle is not putting any stress on the boards. If it is, then additional foam may be required to reduce the angle at which the book is opened. When using a book with detached boards, simply remove the boards from the text block and place them to the side. Cradle the text block sans boards in your cradle.

Examining the Text Block and Leaves

Now that you have your book opened on a cradle, you should examine the condition of the text block. You've already examined the book's fore-edge and spine so you should already have a preliminary sense of the condition of the text block. If you are fully vetting the book, as when the book is newly accessioned, then you should now proceed with a page-by-page examination of the book. If you are simply analyzing the book prior to using it, you may want to look at couple common sites of damage before you continue. If you notice any leaves that appear to be sticking out of the text block, turn to their openings and make sure that these leaves are not loose.

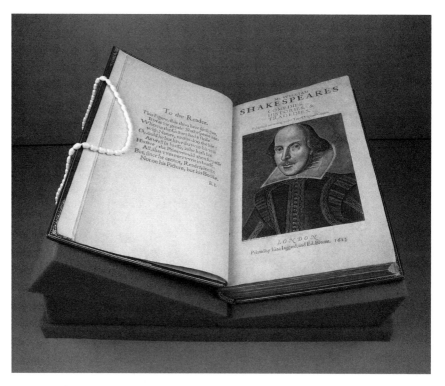

A copy of the First Folio of Shakespeare's works (1623) safely cradled in foam supports and held open by a "snake." (Annie Immediata)

Then carefully make your way to the beginning and end of the book, examining the first and last gatherings of leaves. Because books often circulated for a considerable time without a binding (particularly in the first two centuries of the hand-press era of printing), the first and last gatherings are often sites for wear and tear. Continue to take note of the condition of the fore-edges. It they are brittle, then you will want to be extra careful when turning the pages.

We say "extra careful" because you should already be quite careful when you turn the pages of rare books. Providing instructions on how to turn the pages of a book may seem a little excessive, but significant damage can be caused to rare books through the hasty turning of pages. With this in mind, never turn the pages of a rare book in the same manner that you might turn the pages of the novel that you're reading at home. Also, never fan through the pages of a rare book. This could damage the fore-edges. Besides, there is no need to race through a rare book. As we already have advised: slow down. Before turning a page, examine it. Make yourself aware of any tears or weak spots. Find a strong part to hold and then turn the page. If you need to keep the book opened to a particular page, never do so with your hands. Gently lay a "snake" (a string of lead wrapped in cloth) or a beanbag on the side of the book so that it holds the book open to the pages you need to. If the binding is tight and both sides of the book keep shutting, carefully drape the snake across both pages, so that it holds the entire book open.

A PRESERVATION ENVIRONMENT FOR BOOKS

Thus far we have been discussing the ways to handle a book safely when it is off the shelf and in our hands or a book cradle. Most of the life of the average rare book is not spent in the hands of readers, but rather resting on a shelf. Therefore, librarians and curators must ensure that the environment in which their books are stored is one that will keep the books safe and reduce their natural rate of deterioration.

Getting to Know Your Building and Those Who Maintain It

In their book *The Preservation Program Blueprint*, Barbra Buckner Higginbotham and Judith W. Wild observe:

The library building is the collection's most fundamental source of security, its first line of defense. For this reason, its mechanical systems, maintenance, and other protective qualities are key to the preservation mission. This means that the job of the library building manager is among the most important in the preservation program.[7]

Maintaining a stable environment for your collection is a crucial and challenging responsibility. As Higginbotham and Wild suggest, it is a responsibility shared with, and dependent upon, your library's building manager. Needless to say it is important to forge a good working relationship with that person and his or her staff.

What's more, many of the people who play a role in the preservation of rare books may not necessarily see themselves as a part of that mission. The rare book librarian not only needs to be engaged in constructive professional relationships with the facilities staff, he or she should let them know that they are a part of the library's mission. They need to know your needs, and together you need to be ready for any emergencies. If you are beginning a new job, set up a meeting with your building manager and take the time to learn about your building's history and current environmental needs and challenges.

Temperature and Relative Humidity: Monitoring Your Library's Environment

Creating a healthy environment for rare materials is the challenge of maintaining a healthy and consistent temperature and relative humidity (RH). As Balloffet and Hille observe,

> Since the late 1960s, many preservation specialists have recommended an RH of 50% and a temperature around 60°F (16°C) for storage areas, 24 hours a day, 365 days a year. Frequent fluctuations are harmful to many materials; the key is to *maintain* the desired temperature and RH around the clock, with no major changes.[8]

The U.S. National Archives and Records Administration (NARA) recommends similar temperature and RH standards for paper-based materials: a maximum temperature of 65°F and humidity set points ranging from 35 to 45 percent, with daily fluctuations not exceeding 5°F and/or 5 percent RH.[9] Seasonal fluctuations "must not exceed 5% per month while staying within the +/-5% daily band restriction."[10]

Traditionally, rare book librarians have monitored their library's temperature and RH with hygrothermographs. These devices record temperature and RH 24 hours a day by drawing the levels onto chart paper. Over the last decade, libraries have increasingly switched to digital hygro-thermometers. Library staff should check these devices at least twice a day and record the levels. Any significant fluctuations beyond the recommended ranges mentioned above need to be reported to the facilities/building manager.

Fluctuations in temperature and RH can have significant damaging effects on rare materials. The materials used in the construction of books are hydroscopic, meaning they absorb and release water. During periods of low RH, books release moisture; during periods of high RH, they absorb moisture. Sudden, dramatic changes in temperature and RH put stress on books, as their material pulls and pushes in reaction to releasing or absorbing water. Fluctuation can result in the book's binding and text block bending, shrinking, and buckling. Keeping steady temperature and RH levels will prevent such changes and extend the lives of your books.

The temperature and RH standards suggested above are a good guide, but every library will have their own standards that suit their own distinctive building and collections. In some cases libraries are attempting to find a balance between providing an appropriate temperature for preservation while maintaining an environment that is comfortable enough for the personnel that work in the climate-controlled stacks: 65°F or less is chilly. Whenever possible do not create workspaces in your storage areas. This will free you to set environmental standards with only the collections in mind.

Also, it is important to remember that libraries do not typically have one consistent environment, but many different environments in different parts of the building and within the storage space itself. Greater still are the number of microclimates that exist within your library. They might be found within an exhibition case or within an archival box. Thus you need to choose wisely where you place your hygrothermographs and hygrothermometers.

This is one of the reasons why some libraries have moved to using hygrothermometers that also serve as data loggers that record and store temperature and RH data. Once this data is uploaded to a computer, important information can be extracted from it. The Image Permanence Institute (IPI) at the Rochester Institute of Technology developed one such system with the help of grants from the National Endowment for the Humanities (NEH), the Institute for Museum and Library Services (IMLS), and the Andrew W. Mellon Foundation. Their Preservation Environment Monitors gather data that is organized and interpreted by their Climate Notebook software in a way that provides preservation metrics that analyze and alert you to four potential risks: natural aging, mechanical damage, mold growth, and metal corrosion.

This approach empowers librarians to go beyond just stabilizing the temperature and RH. By studying the data you can determine the possible effects of your storage environment on different kinds of artifacts in your collection. You can also track trends over a longer period of time. Knowing how your building's environment changes throughout the year can help you prepare your facilities staff for adjustments that might have to be made as the weather changes.

HOUSING RARE BOOKS

Some rare books will require some sort of housing or protective structure, because they are in not good enough shape to be stored on the shelf without some sort of stabilization. Other books may demand housing simply because they are rare or unique items that demand further protection. Generally there are three levels of housing.

Level One: Simple Stabilization

Rare book librarians must acknowledge that not every book under their care that is in need of conservation will receive conservation treatment. In most cases, the number of books receiving treatment will be quite low in relation to the size of the collection. A more modest and realistic goal is to stabilize all the items in your collection. We might define "stabilize" as caring for a book in such a way that its condition does not worsen, recognizing, of course, that the materials used to make books are always deteriorating to some extent. On the flip side, stabilization may also mean that the book's condition does not improve. Simple stabilization cannot address major damage in books, but can be used to protect books with the most common damage, such as loose or detached boards, weak joints and hinges, damaged spines, and deteriorating bindings that are in need of refurbishing. There are quick and easy methods to stabilize this sort of damage.

Cloth Ties

The simplest method of holding a book together is by securing it with a cloth tie. For books with loose or detached boards, simply tying an archival-quality cloth tie around the middle of the book like a belt is an easy way of holding the boards to the book. The pros of using cloth ties are that they are cheap and relatively easy to use. A major con of using ties is that if tied too tightly they can damage the edges of the book's boards. Experienced rare book librarians can attest to seeing indentations on bindings caused by years of tight ties. Also, ties can be somewhat tricky to fasten for those who are bad at tying knots (at least one of the authors of this book is hopeless with knots). Struggles with tying knots may be avoided by using cloth ties with plastic fasteners similar to those you might find on the drawstrings of your backpack. Securing the tie with a fastener at the fore-edge eliminates difficult knotting and lessens the risk of pulling the tie too tight. Overall, cloth ties provide a very low level of stabilization at a low price.

Mylar

Another simple and inexpensive way to hold a book together is by using a Mylar band or wrapper. Mylar is an archival-quality film that is quite easy

A cotton tie with a locking fastener is a safe and effective way of stabilizing books with one or both boards detached. (Annie Immediata)

to work with. Instead of using cloth ties, a librarian might stabilize a book by wrapping a Mylar band around its center. The band is usually fastened by Velcro buttons at each end. Although a Mylar band can be gentle on a book and easier to attach than a cloth tie, the Velcro buttons can cause problems. Sometimes the glue holding them to the Mylar loosens, causing the buttons to slide off of the Mylar and stick to the book itself. Sometimes the glue simply dries up and the Velcro buttons fall off. Some institutions fasten the Mylar band with Scotch tape. This isn't a recommended practice. If the tape isn't applied properly, it may end up sticking to the book. Also, if the book is used frequently, the tape securing the Mylar band will have to be replaced frequently.

Mylar can also be used as a wrapper rather than a band. Wrappers are applied the same way as ties, but Mylar wrappers are sized and cut to cover an entire book. Providing more protection for a book than a band, a Mylar wrapper can help stabilize damaged bindings and spines, as well as loose or detached boards. They can also be used to protect bindings. If an early book is bound in a vellum manuscript, for example, then you do not want its binding rubbing up against other books on the shelf, because the ink on that manuscript could end up worn and damaged. A protective Mylar wrapper will help preserve the ink on the manuscript. The downside to Mylar wrappers is the same as those for Mylar bands in that the methods of fastening them can be ineffective. On top of this, you have to be very careful when taking a book wrapped in Mylar off the shelf. If you are holding the book's spine and the Mylar is loose, the book might slide out of its Mylar wrapper, especially if the book is large and heavy or has detached boards. When pulling such a book off the shelf, grip the spine with one hand, while cupping the bottom of the book with your other hand. This way, if the book should slide out of the wrapper, you can catch it. Willie Mays would be proud.

Level Two: Moderate Stabilization

Phase Boxes

Moderate stabilization can be achieved with housing options that are easy enough for librarians who lack conservation training to create and are significantly more effective than simple stabilization techniques. The most common housing is the phase box. The phase box is named as such because it is meant to be only one step or "phase" in a book's conservation process. In this way, the phase box is usually intended to be a temporary housing option used until the book is fully treated and/or moved to a clamshell box (which we will soon describe). The phase box is typically an acid-free card stock or folder stock box that completely encloses a book. This level of protection stabilizes a book suffering from even the most major ailments such as a cracked text block. Guides for making phase boxes and other enclosures from Syracuse University's Special Collections can be found here: http://researchguides.library.syr .edu/content.php?pid=34915&sid=275075

Due to the effectiveness of a well-made phase box, some libraries use them as an option for long-term housing. The Folger Shakespeare Library, for example, has designed a sturdy phase box that is frequently used for long-term housing of books, reserving clamshell boxes for the library's most valuable items. An article describing how to make the Folger phase box appeared in the *Journal of Paper Conservation* in 2011.[11] An interesting feature of this phase box is the use of a Mylar spine. This allows curators and conservators to see the books' bindings while browsing the shelves. Book spines are much more attractive than cardstock, particularly when giving a tour to donors or friends of the library. Having a clear spine is also is a security measure. Simply put, if you cannot see into the box, then you cannot tell at a glance that the book it houses is still inside. If a book is stolen and the box is left behind, you might not realize that the book is missing until a user requests the book and the box is opened.

Envelopes and Slings

Some books are too small or thin to be effectively housed in a phase box. Examples might include pamphlets or short unbound or disbound books.

These types of materials might be better housed in an archival envelope, which can be ordered in various sizes from archival suppliers. The trick is getting the book out of the envelope without damaging it. Reaching into an envelope and pulling out a book is a clumsy process at best. One way to safely remove an item from an envelope is to create a paper sling that is slightly smaller than the size of the envelope. Put the book into the sling, and then slide the sling with the book into the envelope (see illustration). Now, rather than reaching into the envelope and gripping the book, you can grip the sling and gently slide it and the book out together. Items housed in envelopes usually can be shelved upright with the book collection.

Four-Flap Folders

Single-sheet items such as broadsides and printed illustrations should be shelved flat in a housing such as a four-flap folder (see illustration). When closing a four-flap folder, be sure that the large, full flap is the one covering the item. This makes for a more secure housing and eliminates any chance of the edges of the shorter flaps scraping the item. For further protection, a single-sheet item may also be placed in a Mylar sleeve housed in a folder. Having the item enclosed in Mylar allows the users to view both sides of the item, without actually touching it.

Level 3: Long-Term Preservation

A clamshell box provides the greatest, long-term protection for a book. Made from heavy board and stock, it creates a very sturdy enclosure. Note that this means that a bit more width is added to the book and therefore the housed item will take up more shelf space than it would without the enclosure. Construction of clamshell boxes varies from institution to institution. As with their phase boxes, the Folger Shakespeare Library's conservation staff makes clamshell boxes with clear spines. Indiana University Libraries has a terrific illustrated online demonstration on how to make a corrugated clamshell Box: http://iub.edu/~libpres/manual/treatments/corr/index.html. Here's how Cornell University makes their clamshell boxes: http://www.library.cornell.edu/preservation/publications/documents/mg6a.pdf.

SAFELY STORING BOOKS ON SHELVES

Flags and Bookmarks

Books are often shelved with flags containing call numbers, conservation information, warnings of torn pages, etc. If your circulation system is automated, then a flag may also have a barcode attached to it. Limit the number

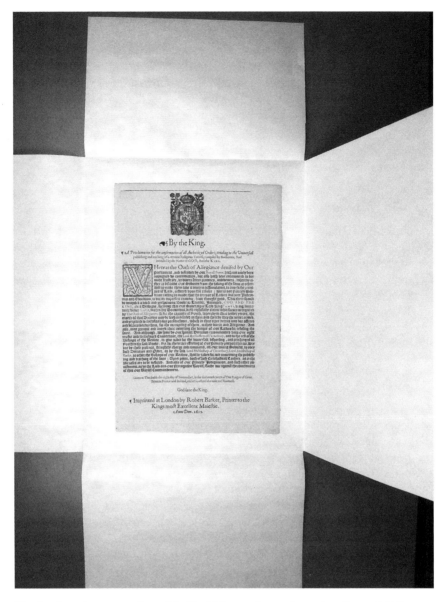

Single-sheet items, such as this English royal proclamation from 1615, may be housed safely in a four-flap folder shelved flat. (Annie Immediata)

of flags kept in a book to two or so, and keep the flags out of the gutter of the book to limit the amount of stress on the book's joints and hinges. Users often wish to put bookmarks in rare books, so keep a supply of archival-quality flags at your circulation desk. Be sure to limit the number of bookmarks users put in a book and do not allow the bookmarks to be left in a book for a long period of time.

Books on Shelves

Bookends, or book supports, come in a variety of types. Libraries often use traditional L-shaped, metal bookends. These can cause trouble. Sometimes the metal can be sharp, potentially causing damage to books. If the tongue of the bookend that slides under the book or books it supports is too thick or sharp, it may cause damage to the bottom of the books' boards. You may want to avoid having books rest atop the tongue of a bookend by using bookends without such a base. A variety of clip-on book ends are available, as are wire book stops. Having a more fixed quality to them, these devices sometimes do not move as easily as traditional bookends, but if you are using a system of shelving spacers like those described above, you will not be moving your bookends very often anyway.

As with all products used in special collections, be sure that your book supports are archival quality. Also make sure that book supports are tall enough so that the books they support do not bend over them. Similarly, a row of books on a shelf needs to be a fairly compact group of similar sizes so that no books tip at an angle or bend over the book next to it. Otherwise the boards of books might become warped and the joints weakened and split. Make sure you and your staff are in the habit of closing up space between books on the shelf and correcting the position of any books that are not shelved properly.

CONSERVATION VERSUS PRESERVATION

The terms "conservation" and "preservation" are often used interchangeably. In their book, *Preservation and Conservation for Libraries and Archives*, Nelly Balloffet and Jenny Hille draw a helpful distinction between the two terms. Conservation may be used to mean the "hands-on-treatment" of a book.[12] Preservation

> encompasses all the steps and activities needed to ensure that the holdings of a library or archive remain in the best possible condition for as long as possible. This includes concerns about storage methods, the building's envelope and environment, security, and other aspects that broadly affect every item in the collection.[13]

Also included in this definition is reformatting as a way of extending "access to information that might be lost once paper or electronic books or documents deteriorate."[14] This includes preserving books digitally, which will be discussed in the next chapter. In a sense, the present chapter has been engaged with principles of preservation, from handling materials properly to making sure that items are transported and housed in a sound and stable manner. For the remainder of the chapter, however, we will discuss conservation.

Rare Book Librarians and Conservators

Although some rare book librarians have training in book and paper conservation, the primary role of the rare book librarian in the conservation process is to identify and prioritize books that need to be treated. Roderick Cave offers a helpful analogy:

> The librarian with experience will be rather like a General Practitioner: well able to diagnose many of the causes of a book's decay, and able to prescribe measures which will prevent or arrest some types of deterioration. But equally he will refer serious cases to a specialist, and leave the subsequent operation to that specialist.[15]

A related analogy is that the librarian performs triage on the wounded books, prioritizing them for surgery.

Depending on their institution, rare book librarians will have varying levels of conservation support. Larger universities and major independent libraries may have their own conservation lab and a staff of conservators, while small colleges or local museums will have to outsource conservation work. In all cases, however, the librarian needs to develop a systematic method of identifying, describing, and prioritizing materials that need to be treated. Many libraries now use a database into which librarians or curators enter and store conservation requests. As the conservators treat a book, they enter information on the treatment and upload images that document their work. This way each database record also serves as a complete record of a book's conservation. This is crucial. Any work done on a book must be documented, whether in a database or in a paper file (hard copies of the database records should be produced and archived, too). This will help future conservators should the need arise to treat a book again. It also ensures that future users know the full extent of the book's history, which is why you should also do your best to conserve books in a way that preserves their historical nature.

Preserving the Book as a Physical Artifact

On the whole, the field of conservation is still relatively young and, in fact, we are currently experiencing the most conscientious conservation era in the history of rare books. Many point to the efforts following the Florence Flood of 1966 as the beginning of the modern field of book conservation. Necessity was the mother of invention as conservators found innovative ways of restoring damaged books and works of art. Within the decades that have followed the flood, the conservation field has blossomed. During the same period of time, scholars have increasingly begun to view books as historical artifacts, influenced by what groundbreaking scholar D. F. McKenzie termed the "Sociology of Texts."[16] We now see value in books that extends well beyond their most simple function as conveyers of textual information. G. Thomas Tanselle beautifully articulated this idea in a recent letter to the editor in *The Times Literary Supplement*:

> Manuscripts and printed books are artefacts; and all artefacts, being physical survivors, give us direct access to parts of a vanished world. They not only carry with them clues to their own production history; they also furnish the basis for reconstructing the visual and tactile experiences that their physical form provided for individuals in the past. The study of both the textual history and the reception of verbal works is dependent on this evidence, which cannot be replaced by any form of reproduction or scholarly report.[17]

The process of book conservation must always take into account each book's history. As Tanselle argues, every book is an artifact containing evidence reflecting the culture that produced it and its life thereafter. Measures must be taken to ensure none of this evidence is lost during treatment, because the artifact itself is the always the preservation copy. As Jim Kuhn from the Folger Library reminds us, "There is information embedded in these objects that will be invaluable to future scholars but that is essentially invisible to us. We devalue the artifact at the future's peril."[18]

Conservation should help preserve artifacts for future generations. If not done properly, however, conservation can have just the opposite effect. In fact, sometimes conservation can erase some or all of a book's history. Not so long ago, for example, when a conservator rebound a book, he or she may have disposed of the original binding. Bindings can, of course, tell us a great deal about a book's history (while in your personal lives it is best not to judge a book by its cover, feel free to do so in your professional lives). These days every effort should be made to preserve the surviving binding, perhaps even rebacking (reattaching) it onto a new covering. If a binding is too damaged for such repairs it may be removed, but it should be kept and housed with the book or in a curatorial file of some sort. The point is to keep treatments as minimal and noninvasive as possible, in order to preserve as much of the original artifact as possible. Also, as mentioned above, a record of the treatments a book receives must be kept, complete with photographs detailing the condition prior to conservation and all the work that was done to it. This way, none of the book's history is lost. You never know what researchers will find important. Some time ago, upon showing a professionally restored copy of the *Nuremberg Chronicle* held by The Ohio State University to a maker of marbled paper, he was less interested in the book itself than the eighteenth-century marbled lining papers that had been saved from an earlier restoration.

The rare book librarian needs to be actively and thoughtfully involved in deciding how a book should be conserved. Be sure that you talk the process through with your conservator and draw up a plan with which you are both comfortable. When in doubt, be sure you are treating the book as a historical artifact. Always err on the side of bibliography.

The Top Five Most Common Book Conservation Treatments

In order to prepare conservation treatment requests, rare book librarians must be familiar with conservation techniques. Described below are the most common injuries to rare books and the appropriate treatments used to repair them. This is a core list meant to provide you with a foundational knowledge of book conservation techniques. As you work with conservators, you will learn much more.

1. Board reattachment. The most common damage you will find in books is detached boards. This is simply because the joints that hold the board onto the text block wear out after decades or centuries of the book being open and shut. Thus it is usually the front board that goes first. Reattaching boards is usually done using one of three methods. Some of these methods could be combined depending on the book's physical structure.
    a. Joint tacketing. The board of a book is sewn back onto the text block. Depending on the height of the book, the conservator chooses three or four areas to sew thread through the book's shoulder (the curved ridge on the length of both sides of the spine) and then through corresponding areas on the spine edge of the board. The thread is pulled and knotted, attaching the board back onto the text block. Japanese paper (Washi) or Korean paper (Hanji) is pasted over the outside joint and inside hinge and toned to match the original cover material/binding or endpaper. In order for this technique to work, the books needs to have a shoulder into which holes can be drilled for the thread. A strong 90° shoulder works best. Joint tacketing is a strong repair, but because holes are drilled into the book's shoulder(s) and board(s), the treatment is the most invasive

technique used for board reattachment. An illustrated article on joint ticketing may be found here: http://cool.conservation-us.org/coolaic/sg/bpg/annual/v10/bp10-08.html.[19]

b. Board slotting. Using a board slotter, the conservator cuts a slot along the spine edge of the board. One edge of a long strip of airplane cotton (a strong cloth) is attached to the spine of the text block (the spine covering may have to be lifted in order to do this). The other side of the airplane cotton strip is inserted into the slot. Thus reattaching the board to the text block. As with joint tacketing, Japanese paper (Washi) or Korean paper (Hanji) is pasted over the outside joint and inside hinge and toned to match the original cover material/binding or endpaper. Board slotting is generally used on thick, heavy boards to ensure a very strong repair. This treatment is best used on thick boards (though not wood) that are square and not beveled. It is fairly invasive. An illustrated article on board slotting may be found here: http://cool.conservation-us.org/coolaic/sg/bpg/annual/v19/bp19-25.html.[20]

c. Airplane cotton bridges. This treatment doesn't have a formal name like the ones above. The conservator uses airplane cotton strips to create a bridge between the spine of the text block and the board. Lifting the leather covering on the head and tail of the spine and board, airplane cotton bridges are inserted, connecting the board to the spine. Connections at the head and tail are crucial because these are the sites of the most stress. Attaching bridges in other areas will depend on where it is easiest to lift the leather. As with the treatments above, Japanese paper (Washi) or Korean paper (Hanji) is pasted over the outside joint and inside hinge and toned to match the original cover material/binding or endpaper. Airplane cotton bridges works best on smaller, lighter books, and are the least invasive and most common technique for board reattachment.

2. Joint repairs. If reattaching boards is the number one treatment, then it makes sense that joint repair would be number two, because joint damage is what leads to a board becoming detached. Wear and tear on the joints is an affliction common to most old books. The simple acts of opening and closing a book's cover slowly lead to a weakening of the joint. When the board is still attached but the joint needs reinforcement or repair, the treatment is much like the final step of board reattachment. The conservator will attach Japanese or Korean paper on top of the joint or, if the leather is easily lifted, attach it underneath (with perhaps a thin strip on top). The paper is then toned to match the original cover material.

3. Paper repair. Damage to the leaves of a book can take various forms including tattered edges, holes (loses), or tears and imperfections in the paper. Books may have such damage but remain stable. But if the damage is preventing a book from being used or is in danger of worsening, then it needs to be repaired.

     a.   Tattered edges. For laid paper (found in pre-nineteenth-century books and modern artists' books), Japanese or Korean paper (or perhaps just its fibers or a very thin tissue paper) is adhered to the edge with gluten-free wheat starch paste (Zin Shofu). For modern wood-pulp paper, a conservator applies heat-set tissue coated with a synthetic adhesive activated with heat.

     b.   Holes (loses). A piece of Japanese or Korean paper shaped to fit the hole is torn in a way that exposes the paper's fiber. It is then adhered over the hole with wheat starch paste. Sometimes the conservator will attach layers of paper to match the thickness of the book's paper.

     c.   Tears. For laid paper, very fine strips of Japanese or Korean paper are adhered over the tears with gluten-free wheat starch paste. For modern wood-pulp paper, a heat-set tissue coated with a synthetic adhesive is used. Tears in which the torn paper still overlaps are pasted together and sometimes reinforced with paper.

4. Binding refurbishment. Rare book librarians will often encounter bindings where the leather is frayed at the corners, peeling off of the boards, or crumbling into dust (creating what is called acidic "red rot"). To consolidate abraded, brittle, and flaky leather, the conservator will apply a mixture of Klucel G (an adhesive) and Ethanol with a small brush in the areas where it is needed. This consolidates the leather without darkening it.

5. Repairing old repairs. As mentioned earlier in this chapter, modern book conservation is really only decades old. However, attempts to repair books extend back centuries. Rare book librarians might now picture in their minds holes in old vellum that have been sewn shut, looking rather like the skin of Frankenstein's monster. These are actually often successful repairs. Others repairs, although made with good intentions, could have negative long-term consequences.

     Perhaps the most common repair that will need fixing is removing strips of often-acidic paper that have been used to repair tears. These paper strips are often also too heavy, making it difficult to turn the page and increasing the risk of further damage. A more shocking approach to fixing a paper tear is to simply tape it together with Scotch tape. You'll be surprised (and perhaps horrified) how often you might encounter this.

     Another common repair that will need updating is a leaf that has been tipped into the book improperly. A single leaf may be "tipped into" a book by applying adhesive paste 2–3 mm along the left edge, lining it up to the text block, and inserting it deep into the gutter. It should be done in a way that allows the leaf to be turned freely. Unfortunately, a bad "tip in" can result in a leaf that bends awkwardly and pulls the page next to it. Such a leaf needs to be reset into the book.

Stuff Found in Books

A careful, noninvasive approach to book conservation also extends to decisions concerning stuff found in books. Every librarian has a tale or two about odd things found in books. Sometimes strange, sometimes valuable, the items left behind tell us something about who has been in possession of the book and how they used the book. We should treat these leftovers as if they were an extension of the physical book. The evidence they provide may prove to be very valuable.

Finding Copernicus

An example that sounds more like something out of a Dan Brown novel than the library world is the story of how rare books helped identify the bones of Nicolaus Copernicus. In 2008, Polish archaeologists found what they thought were the remains of the famous astronomer. DNA was extracted from a remaining tooth and a femur bone, but they needed something with which to match it. They turned to Copernicus's surviving library and found strands of hair in a book that he once owned. The DNA from the hair matched the DNA from the tooth and bone.[21] It's a good thing that the strands of hair remained in that book, and that they had not been blown out or brushed aside by a librarian or reader.

Specimens from an Herbal

Recently, conservators at the Folger Shakespeare Library were treating a copy of John Parkinson's *Theatrum botanicum: The theater of plants* (1640). Pressed within the openings of this herbal were twenty-one specimens that had been inserted by an early owner, a practice not uncommon with herbals. Clearly this flora survives as evidence of how an early reader used the book and should therefore not be discarded. If readers continue to use the book with the specimens in it, however, there is a good chance of losing or damaging the specimens. After consulting with the curatorial staff, the conservators decided to encapsulate each specimen in Mylar, noting the opening from which it had been removed. They then gathered the encapsulated specimens into two boxes that are now shelved alongside the herbal. If a user calls up the herbal, the specimens arrive with it.

These examples present rare book librarians with a pretty weighty challenge. How do we preserve the book as an artifact down to the level of hair and leaves? It reminds us that we need to think critically about every decision we make when conserving our collection. Ultimately, the rare book librarian needs to be thoughtful about how he or she treats surviving stuff found in a book. In most cases it will not need to be encapsulated but just removed to a curatorial file where it can be safely stored. Whenever anything is removed from a book, a note recording the removal and indicating where it is now located should be made in the book's catalog record.

When to Open a Book

Librarians of all backgrounds have at one point or another had a patron present them with an unopened book; i.e., a book with leaves that had never been trimmed and afterward were never opened with a paper-knife and therefore are still attached at the top and perhaps the fore-edge. "Unopened" is the correct term, but "uncut" is sometimes used as well, although it is the term used for books with edges that have not been trimmed.[22] What should you do in this situation?

What's more important: access to the text found in an unopened book or the artifactual value in keeping the book in the condition in which it has survived? In most cases, the latter will be most important and the text the book contains can be found elsewhere. Unopened pages, on the other hand, present evidence of reading that should be preserved. If, for example, the book belonged to a famous owner, it might be important to know that that person did not actually read a specific part of the book.

But what if the book is unique and there are no other resources available to the patron? In some cases, if handled carefully, a user may still be able to read the text of an unopened book. But if the text cannot be read, you need to consider opening the book. If so, do it with the utmost care and document each step you take so that there is a detailed record of what was done. Again, if you are unsure, always err on the side of bibliography. If a book must be opened, however, do not use an instrument with a sharp blade as you risk damage. A letter opener or similar device, used very carefully, is preferred.

Identifying Books for Conservation Treatment

A librarian or conservator usually does not know the current condition of every book in the collection. He or she must rely on colleagues and library users. Indeed, the most common way a book needing conservation is identified is when a user requests a book and the librarian or a member of the circulation staff notices that it is damaged. A similar process occurs when planning an exhibition. Before you put any of your rare materials on exhibit, whether in-house or as a loan to an outside exhibition, you must assess them for any conservation needs. This process ends up identifying many books needing treatment. Another informal way of finding books that need treatment is just by simply browsing your stacks.

A more systematic approach is to conduct a conservation needs survey of your collection or parts of your collection. For large collections a random sample survey would be appropriate; for a smaller collection you could perform an item-level survey. From the survey results you can prioritize books in need of conservation and plan a long-range preservation program. Not many conservation needs surveys for special collections have been published, but for a helpful recent survey, see Jennifer Hain Teper and Sarah M. Erekson, "The Condition of Our 'Hidden' Rare Book Collections," *Library Resources and Technical Services (LRTS)* 50, no. 4 (October 2006): 51–65. In this article the authors detail how they assessed the conservation needs of 20,000 uncataloged items in their collection with a random sample of 4,000 items. Especially useful is the screenshot they provide of the survey interface they designed using the database software Filemaker Pro.

Assessing Newly Acquired Books

As new books are acquired and accessioned, the rare book librarian needs to evaluate their condition. If any new acquisitions are in need of conservation, prepare a conservation report and rehouse and restrict the book as necessary. Reviewing these books should be a page-by-page examination, if possible. Even the most healthy-looking book may have a major tear hidden within its leaves. Such damage should be indicated on a caution flag inserted into the book, so that the next person to use the book knows to take care and does not unintentionally worsen the damage.

But We Cannot Get to Everything ...

Despite the desire of most rare book librarians to care for all of the items in their collections, limited time and resources almost always create a backlog of conservation requests. At times you may feel like a great amount of time is being exerted on writing up treatment reports when it is obvious that the great majority of the collection may never receive treatment. Yet no treatment write-up is a wasted effort, for there is always value in a current condition report. Writing up treatments identifies books that should be restricted for use or used with the help of a librarian. They are also recorded moments in the life of artifacts. They are a part of each book's history.

THE IMPORTANCE OF CONSERVATION
AND PRESERVATION

The books under your care must be preserved for future generations. The way that you handle and store your collections ultimately determines how long they will survive. Best practices may be as simple as handling a book with care, or as advanced as treating a book in the least invasive way with the latest conservation methods. In every case, put the needs of the book first. Remember, too, that you are not alone in the preservation mission. Remind colleagues and library users that they, too, share in the responsibility to ensure the preservation of the collection.

NOTES

1. When a hockey player is said to have "soft hands," it means he or she has excellent stick-handling skills.
2. For more information on the Folger's use of shelving spacers, see Steven K. Galbraith, Linda Hohneke, and Renate Mesmer, "Book Preservation at the Folger Shakespeare Library (1): The Use of Shelf Spacers," *Journal of Paper Conservation* 11, no. 3 (2010): 14–15.
3. Cathleen A. Baker and Randy Silverman, "Misperceptions about White Gloves," *International Preservation News* 37 (2005): 4–16. Available online at: http://www.ifla.org/VI/4/news/ipnn37.pdf.
4. Ibid., 4–5.
5. Ibid., 6.
6. Ibid., 8.
7. Barbra Buckner Higginbotham and Judith W. Wild, *The Preservation Program Blueprint* (Chicago: American Library Association, 2001), 19.
8. Nelly Balloffet and Jenny Hille, *Preservation and conservation for libraries and archives.* (Chicago: American Library Association, 2005), 2.
9. NARA 1571, Archival Storage Standards, February 15, 2002, 13. www.archives.gov/foia/directives/nara1571.pdf.
10. Ibid., 6.
11. Steven K. Galbraith, Linda Hohneke, and Renate Mesmer, "Book Preservation at the Folger Shakespeare Library (2): The Folger Phase Box," *Journal of Paper Conservation* 12, no. 1 (2011): 32–34.
12. Balloffet and Hille, *Preservation and conservation*, xvii.
13. Ibid.
14. Ibid.
15. Roderick Cave, *Rare Book Librarianship* (London: C. Bingley; Hamden, CT: Linnet Books, 1976; rev. ed. London: C. Bingley, 1982), 80.
16. D. F. McKenzie, *Bibliography and the Sociology of Texts* (London: British Library, 1986).
17. G. Thomas Tanselle, "Books as Artefacts," *TLS Letters*, 2 December 2009, http://entertainment.timesonline.co.uk/tol/arts_and_entertainment/the_tls/article6940536.ece, 14 January 2011.
18. Jim C. Kuhn, "re: the Thing Itself," e-mail to Steven Galbraith, 22 June 2009.
19. Robert Espinosa and Pamela Barrios, "Joint Tacketing: A Method of Board Reattachment," *The Book and Paper Group Annual* 10 (1991), http://cool.conservation-us.org/coolaic/sg/bpg/annual/v10/bp10-08.html.

20. Friederike Zimmern, "Board Slotting: A Machine-Supported Book Conservation Method," *The Book and Paper Group Annual* 19 (2000), http://cool.conservation-us.org/coolaic/sg/bpg/annual/v19/bp19-25.html.

21. Adam Easton, "Polish Tests 'confirm Copernicus,' " *BBC News*, 21 November 2008, http://news.bbc.co.uk/2/hi/europe/7740908.stm (16 January 2011).

22. In *ABC for Book Collectors* (New Castle, DE: Oak Knoll Press; London: British Library, 2004), John Carter and Nicolas Barker write, "[unopened] must not be confused, as it often is by philistines, with uncut" (226).

FURTHER READINGS

Appelbaum, Barbara. *Conservation Treatment Methodology*. Amsterdam; Boston: Butterworth-Heinemann, 2007.

Baker, Cathleen A., and Randy Silverman. "Misperceptions about White Gloves." *International Preservation News* 37 (2005): 4–16. Available online at: http://www.ifla.org/VI/4/news/ipnn37.pdf.

Balloffet, Nelly, and Jenny Hille. *Preservation and Conservation for Libraries and Archives*. Chicago: American Library Association, 2005.

McKenzie, D. F. *Bibliography and the Sociology of Texts*. London: British Library, 1986.

NARA 1571, Archival Storage Standards, February 15, 2002. www.archives.gov/foia/directives/nara1571.pdf.

Ogden, Sherelyn. "Temperature, Relative Humidity, Light, and Air Quality: Basic Guidelines for Preservation." Northeast Document Conservation Center (NEDCC), 2007. http://www.nedcc.org/resources/leaflets/2The_Environment/01BasicGuidelines.php.

Teper, Jennifer Hain, and Sarah M. Erekson. "The Condition of Our 'Hidden' Rare Book Collections." *Library Resources and Technical Services (LRTS)* 50, no. 4 (October 2006): 51–65.

CHAPTER 5

Digitization

Digitizing rare materials for access and preservation is one of the most challenging aspects of modern rare book librarianship. The demand for digital access in all its permutations is increasing just as quickly as technology develops and changes. All the while, digitization is a relatively new function for libraries, which are adapting as quickly and effectively as they can. Library users have already adapted. They are expecting to find digital collections online and are disappointed when they do not. While projects such as Google Books may have not set the standard in terms of reproduction quality, they have set an extraordinary standard for access, with searchable full-text (albeit of debatable accuracy) available for books of the machine-press era; and available in increasing quantity for earlier hand-press-era printed works. In the introduction to this book, a case is made for the increasing relevance of special collections in a time when general library collections grow increasingly similar. This can only be true if libraries keep up with demands made by users for access to high-resolution images and, increasingly, access to accurate transcriptions. Thus all librarians must keep up with the latest technology and standards—it is an essential part of the job, and of increasing relevance to rare book libraries. This chapter will focus on what is currently the most common and important digital object in special collections: the digital image.

In the near future, digital access will be an integral part of the day-to-day operation of special collections libraries. Much like reference services or interlibrary loan, user requests for digital images of rare materials are already more and more becoming a free, or self-service, offering for the library's communities. A variety of models are in the process of being worked out even now, either via absorbing the cost for providing these services as a part of the general operating budget, or through encouraging users to capture the images they need of collection material with either their own cameras or with dedicated library equipment. Though wide adoption of such changes is still in the near future, libraries need to begin now in planning for and establishing best practices for the coming transformation of traditional reading room services.

Providing facsimiles of special collections material is not a new concept, nor is it limited to digital surrogates. Digital imaging is just the latest technology. Libraries have long produced facsimiles in a variety of media, many of which are still in use today and will continue to be used. Thus we begin this chapter with a review of the more common imaging formats and the ways in which digital technology is supplanting them. Please note that in this chapter we are primarily concerned with the digitization of books and other printed materials. Depending on your collection, digitization could extend to other media such as audio and video; as well as the creation and maintenance of libraries of optical character recognition (OCR)-based or rekeyed transcriptions of printed materials.

TRADITIONAL SERVICES AND FORMATS

Facsimile reproductions of rare materials have traditionally been rendered in three principal formats: microfilm (and other microformats), photocopies, and film photography. Of these three, photocopying is the most common service. It is expected in libraries and can be used for most materials in good enough condition to be placed "face down" and flat on a photocopier. Library users typically use photocopies (or, increasingly, pdf scans made at photocopy machines) for research when they need long-term access to information or have only limited time available to spend in library reading rooms. Libraries occasionally keep photocopied versions of rare materials as facsimiles for users. Sometimes they are bound and shelved with the circulating collection. In these cases, photocopies have some archival value, but on the whole, photocopying is not used for that purpose. Film photography of rare materials has been common in the past as a means of providing researchers with color reproductions, or when an item has been deemed too fragile to be photocopied. Film photography was also typically the medium used when researchers needed illustrations for their publications. In this case, the library may have kept a negative or copy of the photograph for archival purposes and for use in fulfilling future orders.

Photocopy and film photography services are both fee-based. Photography is staff-intensive (and is sometimes outsourced); photocopying is typically left to the users. As in the general population, so in the library community: film photography has essentially been superseded by digital photography. And although the lights of photocopiers still regularly flash in most libraries, users are increasingly choosing to photograph objects with their own digital cameras rather than take a photocopy. Not only is it convenient, it saves the user money, and with the right policies in place may in fact save the library wear and tear on its collection materials.

Microfilm has played a more archival role in libraries and continues to do so in many collections. Microfilm also extends access, whether through libraries acquiring large collections of books or manuscripts reproduced in microfilm sets or researchers ordering a microfilm copy of an artifact for personal use. Although it is not a favorite of users, microfilm facsimiles take up little space, are relatively inexpensive, are an archivally stable format, and can be viewed with optical magnification technology that has itself been stable for decades and is therefore unlikely to be rendered obsolete in the near future. Nevertheless, in the digital age the creation of microfilmed collections is growing more and more rare.

And yet issues of format longevity are not quite so clear with digital content, which increasingly is rendered or stored in formats that have not been tested in the same way that paper and microformats have been. Many digital formats have proven to be ephemeral, particularly CDs and DVDs, which should be used only as transportation media and not for long-term storage. Thus librarians need to keep up with standards concerning digital reproduction and storage. We will say more on this topic later in this chapter. For now we need to repeat something that we stated elsewhere in this book: no digital surrogate, no matter how high the resolution or seemingly secure, can ever replace the actual artifact. It is a good practice to make facsimiles of rare or fragile materials, but the continued conservation of the artifact itself is of the utmost importance.

DIGITAL IMAGING AND ACCESS

For users, the need for digital images of rare materials usually falls into one of two categories. The first is a request for an image or set of images for the purpose of study. The second is a request for an image or set of images for the purpose of publication. In the first instance, the user needs an image that is good enough for research purposes, though perhaps not of publishable quality. The user might settle for a photocopy if it were permitted, but upending a rare book onto the glass of a photocopier and making copies is rarely a good idea. Digital cameras are now filling the need for a working copy that a photocopier once filled, as users increasingly take photographs with their own digital cameras while examining books in library reading rooms.

Digital Cameras in the Reading Room

Researchers have come to expect that they will be able to use their digital cameras to make reproductions of the materials that they are studying. Although the majority of libraries allow digital cameras in their reading rooms (and a number more will, too, by the time this book is published), some still have resisted, but to their own disadvantage. Not only does allowing digital cameras in the reading room improve user satisfaction, it is beneficial to the collection in a number of ways. Done properly, digital photography is much easier on the materials than repeated use or photocopying. Once the user has a digital facsimile of the item, he or she will likely not need to view the item repeatedly, but will study their personal facsimile. A reduced need for photocopying results in a decreased consumption of paper and toner. This is a benefit to our environment, but if photocopying was a stream of revenue, then the library will have to work out how to make up for the monetary loss. Most institutions charge a reproduction fee if their staff creates a digital image for a user. Some institutions even charge users who take digital photographs. That is not recommended, nor will these policies last long. If institutions do charge for digital access, they should do so in accordance with the principles laid out it in the ALA/SAA Joint Statement on Access to Research Materials in Archives and Special Collections Libraries:

> Repositories should strive to provide access to their holdings at no direct cost to the researcher. In situations where this is not possible, reasons for charging fees should be made publicly available. A repository should facilitate access to collections by providing reasonably priced reproduction services that are administered consistently in accordance with legal authority, including copyright law, institutional access policy, and repository regulations. These services may include electronic, paper, or photographic copies; microfilm; or other means of reproduction and should be clearly stated in a publicly accessible written policy.[1]

These progressive recommendations anticipate a time when digital access will be a free service for users. In the meantime, charging a fee is understandable, so long as it is done sensibly.

Although cutting into an existing revenue stream, allowing users to take their own photographs for research purposes should cut down on the number of photography requests, thus reducing staff workload and allotting more time to digitize items in your ongoing imaging stream. Also, as Miller and Galbraith note in their report, "Digital cameras reduce liability for copyright infringement," because "when a repository makes copies of copyrighted documents for users or provides equipment on which users can make their own copies, it runs the risk of engaging in direct and indirect copyright infringement."[2] Ironically, a hands-off approach to cameras in the reading room may lessen a library's risk for copyright liability.[3]

Allowing digital cameras in reading rooms can be a positive policy, but your own institutional guidelines must be clearly written and apparent. At a 2008 RBMS preconference seminar titled "Digital Photography on a

Budget," Stanford University's Mattie Tamora shared her experiences implementing a policy for digital cameras in the reading room and bore witness to the fact that users treat books differently as photographers than they do as readers. One might wonder why camera-use policies specifically preempt behavior such as standing on chairs or laying books on the ground, but readers have been known to do such unthinkable things in an effort to get a good shot of the object. Such rules are reactions to actual behavior.

But for 99 percent of cases, guidelines for user photography will be pretty much the same as book-handling guidelines. Additions may include turning off the camera's sound and flash (more because it is disruptive to other readers than potentially harmful to most objects) and not allowing users to photograph the reading room, library staff, or other users.[4] The OCLC Research report " 'Capture and Release': Digital Cameras in the Reading Room" presents suggested practices for allowing cameras in the reading room and a grid of potential policies that your library could adopt. Also included is a modular "Camera Use in Reading Room" permission form that libraries can adapt to their own needs.[5]

Publication-Quality Images

If a user requests an image or set of images for print publication, then the image needs to be taken at a higher, publication-ready resolution. In this case, it may make sense for the institution to take an archival-quality image that can also be housed in the library's digital collection. Depending on the rarity or fragility of the item, it might also make sense to digitize the whole item for archival purposes, even if the user has requested only a page or several pages. Indeed, most digital requests will be for one or two pages, rather than a whole book. This is what some refer to as the trouble with "one-sies and two-sies."[6] While every librarian wishes he or she could digitize the whole of every item that is requested, time and resources usually do not allow for it. Your library needs to take the time to draw up a digitization workflow that articulates what standards should be used for different types of requests and when requested items might be fully digitized, or digitized at a very high resolution. In fact, there may be categories of material (e.g., scrapbooks of newspaper clippings); or categories of requests (e.g., images for use online or images requested only to provide access to intellectual content) that justify policies and workflows aimed at low-resolution use copies. Regardless, all digitization workflows should—as permitted by conservation requirements—be as streamlined as possible. A recently published OCLC research document, "Scan and Deliver: Managing User-Initiated Digitization in Special Collections and Archives," provides guidance to libraries of all sizes on how they can design and manage digitization workflows to meet their own needs and types of user requests.[7]

DIGITAL IMAGING AND THE NEEDS OF THE LIBRARY

Digitization is primarily an access medium though it plays a direct role in promoting preservation efforts. Although user requests for digital images help build a digital library, librarians should also have a digitization stream for items and collections that are strong candidates for having a digital surrogate. Behind this digitization stream should be a queue of items that staff have selected. Determining factors could be the rarity of the item, the frequency with which the item circulates, and its physical condition. If a frequently consulted book begins to show signs of wear, then that book would be a good candidate for digitization. Users can then be directed to the digital copy rather than book itself. This should satisfy most researchers, although those who work on books as material objects and other related topics might need to consult the original. Depending on the resources at your disposal, your digitization stream may be conservative or ambitious. On the one hand, it may be that staff time or equipment or budgetary constraints only allow for the occasional digitization in full of specific books or other collection material. In that case, be very selective about what you chose to preserve. On the other hand, if a library has ample resources or is willing to engage in relatively quick, low-resolution imaging, a more ambitious policy could be to digitize all new acquisitions. Digitization policies and workflows will be as diverse as the libraries and user communities they serve.

Digitizing Unique and Rare Items

One way to begin a digitization program is by identifying the unique and very rare items in your collection. Just as libraries have preserved unique and rare items in microfilm and other traditional formats, they should continue to do so through digitization. Begin with unique items for which there is no existing facsimile. These are at the greatest risk. If lost, stolen, or destroyed, the information they contain could be gone forever. Researchers are often dissatisfied with having to use facsimiles and often can be dismissive of the practice of creating them. Yet there are examples in which the original artifact has gone missing or was destroyed, and our only access to the information that artifact carried is through facsimiles. Thus the value of facsimiles should never be underestimated.

Digitizing Popular Items

No matter how carefully library staff and users handle rare books, the condition of frequently used books will slowly worsen over time. It is not just the opening of the book and the turning of its pages. Every time a book is called up, it has to be taken off the shelf, brought to the circulation desk, and delivered to the user. When the user is done working with the book, it

The Importance of Facsimiles

In an essay titled "Lost: The Destruction, Dispersal, and Rediscovery of Manuscripts," Peter Beal reminds us of the magnitude of the information that has been lost, but also notes what information has been saved via facsimiles of books and manuscripts that are no longer extant.[10] By way of an example, he points to the unique copy of the play *Sir Thomas More*, which famously survives in a manuscript containing the hands of several Elizabethan playwrights, possibly including William Shakespeare.[11] The amount of use this manuscript has received, coupled with "incompetent 'conservation' " has caused it to deteriorate to the extent that several lines written by "Hand D" (the hand possibly belonging to Shakespeare) are no longer legible. Fortunately, Shakespeare scholar W. W. Gregg preserved these lines by recording them in his early-twentieth-century edition of the play.[12]

takes the same journey back to the shelf, all the while being handled by staff. Throughout these two trips, the chances of an accident befalling the book increase. The more popular a book, the more often it travels and is handled. The books that circulate most in your collection are possible candidates for digitization. No matter what the collection, there will be a core group of books that receive the most use, reflecting Richard Trueswell's famous "80/20 rule" that suggests that 20 percent of a library collection circulates 80 percent of the time.[8] If you have an electronic circulation system, identifying popular books for digitization is simply a matter of outputting your statistics. Even if you do not have such a system, a hands-on librarian knows the books that circulate more often than others and can also seek suggestions from colleagues, particularly those working at the circulation desk.

Digitizing Fragile Materials

Books that are too damaged or fragile to be handled without causing further damage are often restricted for use. Their contents, therefore, are not accessible to researchers. In some cases a facsimile of the book may exist in some form and therefore the user may have intellectual access to the book. If, however, a book needed by a user is restricted because of its condition and there is not an existing facsimile (or there isn't another copy at an accessible library), then that book may be a candidate for digitization. Otherwise, your user may not have any access to its contents. Every library will own a number of books that are restricted because of condition. Digitizing all of these books is usually not an option; in fact, some may be too fragile to be digitized at all. One way to prioritize collection material that is restricted because of condition is to track how often users request them. If your damaged

---

Digitizing Shakespeare's Quartos

In 2008 and 2009 the Folger Shakespeare Library teamed up with Oxford University to create the Shakespeare Quartos Archive (SQA), which provides online access to 32 digitized and fully transcribed copies of *Hamlet*. Part of this grant-funded project was also the digitization of all pre-1641 copies of all Shakespeare plays and poems at the Bodleian Library of the University of Oxford, the British Library, the University of Edinburgh Library, the Folger Shakespeare Library, the Huntington Library, and the National Library of Scotland. Copies of early Shakespeare quartos are quite rare and sometimes unique, as in the case of the Folger's 1594 edition of *Titus Andronicus*. Digitizing these books not only helps preserve them for future generations by minimizing use, it facilitates worldwide access to them. Shakespeare's quartos are the subject of a significant amount of research and are frequently requested by researchers. If these quartos circulated as often as they were requested, their condition would slowly deteriorate, no matter how carefully they were handled. Digital surrogates available freely online provide a level of access that is acceptable to most researchers, while lengthening the lifespan of the artifacts. See: The Shakespeare Quartos Archive, http://www.quartos .org, and Shakespeare in Quarto, http://www.bl.uk/treasures/shakespeare/ homepage.html.

---

books are given attention flags with instructions not to remove them from the shelf, then you might note the dates on which the item was requested on the back of the flag. If the number of requests adds up, you've got a good candidate for digitization.

Safely Digitizing Material

The process of digitizing books needs to have as little impact on the condition of the books as possible. The good news is that unless books are in particularly poor condition, they should be relatively easy to digitize safely. The rules of handling a book during digitization are basically the same as handling a book for research, though, as noted above, one has to remain cautious when switching gears from librarian to photographer. The desire to get a good shot should not get in the way of a book's safety.

Before digitization begins, the condition of the book needs to be evaluated by a librarian, curator, conservator, or another trained member of your staff, depending on the workflow that you have created. Evaluate the book just as you would whenever you are assessing a book's condition (suggested practices may be found in Chapter 4). During the evaluation keep an eye open for the most severe damage such as cracked spines and brittle and torn pages. Also be mindful of delicate bindings such as embroidered and velvet bindings, and tight text blocks that are difficult to keep open past 45 degrees or so. There are numerous such examples that might disqualify a book for digitization, but there might also be some hope for them. In certain cases, you might choose to have a damaged or fragile book conserved and stabilized before being photographed. In others, you might have a book digitized at an appropriate stage of conservation. For example, if the conservator plans to disbind a book and pull (i.e., disassemble) the text block, this might present an opportunity to scan each individual leaf before the text block is sewn back together. All in all, if a book is worth digitizing, then there may be ways to make that happen. Once it is digitized, of course, your users will have intellectual access to it via facsimile images, with the book remaining undisturbed in the vault.

The most efficient way to digitize a book is to photograph each opening in a two-page spread. In order to do this, the book must be able to be opened at 160 degrees or so, but without putting undue stress on the text block, spine, or boards. Fortunately, most high-end cameras can shoot a book that is not opened flat and still not lose any of the text that runs into the gutter. The field of depth can be software-corrected, creating an image that appears fairly flat. If a book cannot be opened far enough to facilitate a two-page spread, then, for the safety of the book, it must be shot one page at a time in a cradle. This process can be made easier by using a cradle to which a camera can be attached to one side or the other. With a single camera you would shoot all of the verso pages and then move it to the other side of the cradle to shoot all of the recto pages. Your images will be out of signature order, but a simple computer program can gather the files back into order. Remember that digitizing books will often have limitations. Every book will be different from the next and you must make do with the challenges each book presents.

The quality at which you shoot your images may depend on the nature of the request. Has a reader requested a working copy or a publication quality copy? Is the image being published online or being reproduced in a book? Perhaps your library needs to produce an archival-quality copy for preservation. Unless it is your policy to shoot all images at archival quality, your approach may change for each scenario. Your decision may also depend on how much room you have to store your images. Archival quality images take up a great deal of space very quickly.

Flat items such as broadside proclamations or maps are perhaps the easiest to digitize, because they only need to be placed flat on a flatbed scanner. A scan may take longer than a camera shot, but most flat items require only one or two scans. Flat items do not require a cradle or a camera, so they may be digitized concurrently with a book being photographed in a cradle. One concern about flatbed scanners may be the intensity of the scanner light and the length of time the item is exposed to it. This light is more direct and more intense than a photoflash, so the condition of the item should be taken into consideration. In most cases flatbed scanning is a relatively safe process.[9]

THE CHALLENGES OF DIGITIZATION

The more a library can digitize, the better for access and collection preservation, but there are major challenges in keeping up with standards concerning how you create, describe, and store content. Due to the evolving nature of technology, digitization standards are a continuing conversation. Each library needs to define their standards concerning file format, bit depth, and resolution in line with the current best practices and the needs of their users. Your digitization policy and standards should address how much descriptive metadata (i.e., data about the item being digitized) and administrative metadata (i.e., data about the digital image itself) you want to associate with your digital content. As with digitization, you may have different metadata standards for different content and different users. An archival digital image might carry with it robust metadata, while a lower-quality image for personal use or research might have the most elemental descriptive metadata. Also keep in mind that depending on the item and the digitization or metadata workflows involved, the process of digitization may be faster than the creation of the metadata.

Many special collections institutions post their digitization, metadata creation, and storage standards online, which can easily be found with a web search. As you create and update your own policies, you will have many strong examples online to guide you. Also, for guidance on the latest digitization standards and on digital preservation, you can consult the resources at the Federal Agencies Digitization Guidelines Initiative: http://www .digitizationguidelines.gov/ and Digital Preservation program at the Library of Congress, http://www.digitalpreservation.gov/.

If your library is making the investment to produce archival-quality images (or even simply high-resolution images), then the logical next step is to create an online database so that local and distance users can access your content. There are a surprising number of ways to put digitized materials online. Some libraries create their own digital libraries that are housed on internal or outsourced servers and accessible through their website using a custom or open-source interface or through proprietary software. Choices may depend on such factors as how much in-house support they have to maintain the site versus how much budgetary freedom exists to outsource hosting year after year, along with how much control they want to have over their content. The downside to such approach is that the collection might end up somewhat hidden unless an institution is actively engaged in outreach; e.g., through the Open Archives Initiative (OAI-PMH) or deliberate exposure and submission of sites to search engine crawls. Other libraries upload digital images onto public sites like Flickr. Institutions such as the Library of Congress, the National Archives and Records Administration, the National Galleries of Scotland, and Smithsonian Institution have contributed to Flickr Commons in an effort to both share their content and to have the public share what information they might have about the content. Thus this is also an example of generating social metadata. (For more on this see Chapter 10, Part 2). Sites such as Flickr have become popular destinations for users looking for images. Placing your content on well-trod websites is a good example of *meeting your users where they are* as opposed to working to bring them to your website. It is important to limit the number of steps it takes to get the content. Online users have come to expect instant access. Steps such as registering for accounts and logging in, though seemingly innocuous, are hassles for users.

The greatest investment in digitization is in the IT infrastructure required to maintain access over time. When master images are produced at archival quality they can be around 100MB for each image, with first derivatives around 80MB. For example, the total file-size of a high-resolution digital copy of the Shakespeare First Folio of 1623, is approximately 45GB at the Folger Shakespeare Library and that is shooting about 900 pages as double page spreads (so shooting one page at a time would approximately double that size). In today's library, digital storage and server space is just as important as shelf space. Make sure you have both storage space and tested backup plans for your current digitization goals and continue to plan for future growth.

For long-term preservation, you may wish to use one of the many collaborative or vendor-based digital preservation services. Some of these services are dark archives (e.g., MetaArchive and Chronopolis), meaning they store files but do not provide user access to them. Thus the content of these archives is hidden from public view. These archives typically ensure the longevity of your content in part by storing it in several different geographical locations to prevent loss from natural disasters and other such events, so content may be stored in four to six different geographical locations. They should also regularly check your files for any data loss. Other preservation services are light archives, meaning they provide both preservation and access to your content (e.g., Ex Libris Rosetta). If you are working in a university or college library, you may have a shared institutional repository for archiving digital content and making it available on an ongoing basis. Whatever you choose, make sure that the content you are spending so much time and money to produce is going to have as long a life as possible.

THE IMPORTANCE OF DIGITAL ACCESS AND PRESERVATION

The digital component of rare book librarianship is probably the most challenging at the moment. On top of traditional skills and expertise, librarians must now keep up with the ever-changing world of digital access and preservation. Doing so can be as daunting as it is exciting, but the rewards are manifold. Through the process of making your materials accessible on-line, you can help minimize use of the artifacts, thereby preserving them for future generations and for research requiring direct access to the physical object. Digital images are primarily geared toward access to intellectual content, but the value of high-resolution facsimiles cannot be underestimated, so long as they are safely stored. As we will see in Chapter 10, having your materials online opens the door for the application of various social media and the encouragement of social metadata supplied by your users. You are serving your users best when you are meeting their needs and meeting them where they are. They are online. And you need to be, too.

NOTES

1. ALA/SAA Joint Statement on Access to Research Materials in Archives and Special Collections Libraries, adopted by the SAA Council on June 1, 2009, and the ACRL Board during the ALA Annual Conference, July 2009: http://www.archivists.org/statements/ALA-SAA-Access09.asp and http://www.ala.org/ala/mgrps/divs/acrl/standards/jointstatement.cfm.

2. Lisa Miller, Steven K. Galbraith, and the RLG Partnership Working Group on Streamlining Photography and Scanning, "'Capture and Release': Digital Cameras in the Reading Room," report produced by OCLC Research, 2010. Published online at http://www.oclc.org/research/publications/library/2010/2010-05.pdf.

3. For more on copyright issues, see Peter B. Hirtle, Emily Hudson, and Andrew T. Kenyon, *Copyright and Cultural Institutions: Guidelines for Digitization for U.S. Libraries, Archives, and Museums* (Ithaca, NY: Cornell University Library, 2009), 78–83, http://hdl.handle.net/1813/14142.

4. For a thorough study on the effects of light on various materials, see Terry T. Schaeffer, *Effects of Light on Materials in Collections: Data on Photoflash and Related Sources* (Los Angeles: Getty Publications, 2001).

5. Miller, Galbraith, and the RLG Partnership Working Group on Streamlining Photography and Scanning, "Capture and Release."

6. The expression "one-sies and two-sies" become popular after it was used by Janice Ruth of the Library of Congress in the Q & A section of a panel titled "Going with the Flow: Sustainable Models for Integrating Digitization" at the annual meeting of the Society of American Archivists in 2009.

7. Jennifer Schaffner, Francine Snyder, and Shannon Supple, "Scan and Deliver: Managing User-Initiated Digitization in Special Collections and Archives" (Dublin, OH: OCLC Research, 2011), http://www.oclc.org/research/publications/library/2011/2011-05.pdf.

8. Richard W. Trueswell, "Some Behavioral Patterns of Library Users: The 80/20 Rule," *Wilson Library Bulletin* 43 (1969): 458–61.

9. If you have questions concerning the effects of light on your materials, see Terry T. Schaeffer, *Effects of Light on Materials in Collections: Data on Photoflash and Related Sources*. Los Angeles: Getty Publications, 2001.

10. See Peter Beal. "Lost: the Destruction, Dispersal, and Rediscovery of Manuscripts," in *Books on the Move: Tracking Copies through Collections and the Book Trade*, ed. Robin Myers, Michael Harris, and Giles Mandelbrote (New Castle, DE: Oak Knoll Press, 2007).

11. British Library Harleian MS 7368.

12. Peter Beal. "Lost: the Destruction, Dispersal, and Rediscovery of Manuscripts," 7.

FURTHER READINGS

ALA/SAA Joint Statement on Access to Research Materials in Archives and Special Collections Libraries, adopted by the SAA Council on June 1, 2009, and the ACRL Board during the ALA Annual Conference, July 2009, accessed February 1, 2010, at http://www.archivists.org/statements/ALA-SAA-Access09.asp and http://www.ala.org/ala/mgrps/divs/acrl/standards/jointstatement.cfm. Although access is discussed in a broad sense, digital preservation and access are key parts of the statement.

Blue Ribbon Task Force on Sustainable Digital Preservation and Access. Final Report, February 2010. 29 September 2011. http://brtf.sdsc.edu/index.html.

Digipres, http://lists.ala.org/wws/info/digipres. An ALA listserv focusing on digital preservation.

Dooley, Jackie. "Ten Commandments for Special Collections Librarians in the Digital Age." *RBM: A Journal of Rare Books, Manuscripts, and Cultural Heritage* 10, no. 1 (Spring 2009): 51–59.

Miller, Lisa, Steven K. Galbraith, and the RLG Partnership Working Group on Streamlining Photography and Scanning. " 'Capture and Release': Digital Cameras in the Reading Room." Report produced by OCLC Research, 2010. Published online at http://www.oclc.org/research/publications/library/2010/2010-05.pdf.

Savage, Bryn. "Rare Book Photography: An Introduction." Yale University. http://bibliofile.commons.yale.edu/files/2011/08/RareBooks12.pdf

Schaeffer, Terry T. *Effects of Light on Materials in Collections: Data on Photoflash and Related Sources*. Los Angeles: Getty Publications, 2001. Schaeffer's work is a thorough study on the effects of light on various materials.

CHAPTER 6

Security and Disaster Preparedness

Security and disaster preparedness are absolutely essential components for a well-operated rare book or special collections library. In the most direct and clearest statement, a missing book is no book, and a severely damaged book can be close to useless. Sadly, we must all accept our mortality, but, more optimistically, we can expect that books and manuscripts, given the proper attention and protection, are nearly immortal. Rare book librarians are committed to protect and administer the collections under their charge. Regardless of good public service, expeditious and thorough cataloging, extensive and fruitful outreach and promotion, or any other aspect of rare book librarianship, if the books are lost or destroyed, all these admirable activities are for naught.

THEFT AND MALICIOUS DAMAGE

All aspects of rare book librarianship are contingent upon the protection of the materials in the collection. Security of materials necessitates planning for unpleasant possibilities: stealing of books, switching of books, marring of books, and mishandling of books, to broach the most obvious incidents. The literature on theft and damage of library materials is extensive. Essential reading includes the documents from the RBMS Security Committee of the Rare Books and Manuscripts Section of ALA at http://www.rbms.info/committees/security/index.shtml.

The history of theft in libraries demonstrates its pervasiveness and emphasizes the need of constant vigilance.[1] The book thief cannot be stereotyped and traverses age, race, gender, class, and profession. Sadly, all too frequently, book thieves are "trusted patrons." For instance, among college and university libraries, faculty have an unenviable history of book theft. Even more sadly, the most common instance of book theft involves library staff. In the same way that all library users and staff, regardless of external status, should be treated with equally courtesy and respect, so, too, they should all be monitored with equal vigilance.

This is the dark side of rare book librarianship, where realities must be faced. The librarian, like a detective, must think of motive and modus operandi, must be a Sherlock Holmes to the Professor Moriarty of book thieves. First and foremost, in the area of public service, dual coverage of the rare book reading room is virtually a universal application that guarantees a book is never left unattended with a patron. Obviously, a theft can only occur when an item is available to the thief, and a simple request to view a rare book may be the first step in that process. For instance, a common pattern of book theft documented through the ages involves the trusted patron—faculty, scholar, researcher—known to library staff, respected by colleagues, renowned in his or her field. For the matter of illustration, the patron may be consulting manuscript leaves, and, with the usual restrictions of rare book usage, must view the materials within a restricted area and within limited hours. At the end of the day, the assiduous researcher still has more to investigate and one day slips a single manuscript leaf into his briefcase so that he can take it home to explore it in more detail. Again, this is a demonstrated pattern, but even if it occurs only once, that is one time too many. There may not have been any premeditation, rather, an act of impulse, and the item even returned, but, with that success the pattern continues until one time the material is not returned.

Rare materials are particularly vulnerable because, tautologically, these materials are indeed rare or even unique to an institution, region, or nation. Someone may want an item for its monetary value, but others may want it for its personal value for research or sheer possession. The most notorious book thief of the twentieth century, Stephen Blumberg, did not steal millions of dollars' worth of books to sell, but rather to hoard in his Victorian house in Ottumwa, Iowa.[2] And though the most valuable of books within a rare book library are typically most guarded, it cannot be precluded that lesser items may not be equally desired and vulnerable for a variety of reasons far too numerous to list here. Again, based on experience, we can cite the case of a paperback text being taken via a switch. Was the paperback of great monetary value? Not particularly, but it was a copy unique to a large research library. A patron requested the item and returned a similar item and left the reading room quickly. Obviously, this was premeditated. Upon examination of the patron's name, it was discovered to be phony, and it demonstrated a lapse in checking for personal identification.

Beyond theft, there is also the possibility of damage or destruction of rare book materials. Controversial political, religious, or erotic texts, for example, are always vulnerable to patrons who harbor extreme personal agendas and feel that certain ideas contained within such texts endanger the welfare of others or offend a creed. Historically, there are instances of Catholic references being crossed out in Puritan texts and vice versa, and book bans or, more extreme, book burnings by intolerant groups. Somewhat recently, the publication of Salmon Rushdie's *Satanic Verses* and the subsequent fatwa issued by the Ayatollah Khomeini in 1988 initiated the transfer of that book to the rare books department in no small number of libraries. Should a patron be intent upon damage or destruction of such an item, realistically such an incident could occur rapidly even under the most rigorous invigilation, but such a possibility does not exempt as careful supervision of materials as possible.

As noted, dual coverage of the reading room remains the single most important security component for rare book materials, but there are other measures to ensure further protection. Most individuals who might contemplate theft or damage of materials do not wish to be detected. A log of every patron using materials not only provides an official record but also acts as a deterrent. The log is effective, of course, only if identification is required to confirm that the name on the log is, indeed, the name of the person signing in. This is not to suggest that serious thieves cannot fabricate fake identification—they can. This is only to say that the greater the scrutiny of the rare book library the lesser the opportunity for theft.

Preventative Measures

Additional preventative measures against theft, such as security cameras, alarm systems, and "buzz-in" doors, are highly desired but are dependent upon institutional resources. Other precautions under the control of the local rare book library, regardless of institutional resources, include prohibition of briefcases, book bags, and purses at the reading tables. Pencils only is a common requirement in most rare book reading rooms and prevents indelible markings in texts. The use of laptop computers has become commonplace, though precise policy on such matters will differ with each rare book library, as many institutions have patrons open their laptops up before they exit to show that nothing has slipped inside.[3] The amount of material used at any given time can be limited to a single book or folder. In the case of a folder of manuscript leaves there should be an accounting of leaves before and after use: such a process protects not only the materials themselves, but also the patron who may have received a folder that was missing a leaf, taken prior to its use. Some libraries weigh materials on a sensitive scale before giving them to a patron, and then weigh them again when they are returned. If anything has been removed there will be a discrepancy in weight.[4]

Although it may seem antiquated in the automated world of the twenty-first century, some form of paper record remains an effective means for the monitoring of book use, and particularly as an added security measure for the protection of the materials in addition to assurance for the patron. Certainly, the advent of automated circulation systems for individual rare book collections augments and streamlines record keeping, but the paper form is an added security measure that can help facilitate the physical operation of a rare books reading room in a way that the automated system cannot. For instance, a common triplicate paper form provides for a shelf marker when a book is retrieved, a monitor of current use, and a receipt for the patron. The shelf marker expedites reshelving, the monitor form becomes another record of use, and the receipt form is evidence for the patron of return of the material.

As with all advice, the stringencies of public policy will be unique to each institution. For instance, your library may likely have a designated security officer with whom you should consult on a regular basis. If the rare book librarian should be the designated security officer, you should assemble a security and disaster preparedness committee to establish policies and procedures for emergency situations. Also, despite the strictest of policies, exceptions may occur to facilitate access and scholarship. For instance, a textual scholar may have to compare multiple states of a text thus requiring use of more than one book at a given time.

Although theft is the preeminent component in security planning, destruction of materials is also a risk as alluded to in the case of controversial texts. Yet, unintentional damage can also occur and every precaution should be taken to limit such possibilities. It may be assumed that everyone knows how to handle rare and sometimes fragile materials, but such is not the case. Although instruction in the handling of books and manuscripts may seem tedious, it is necessary. Certainly, if any mishandling of materials is observed, remediation should be immediate. It cannot be over-emphasized that the rare book librarian is the steward of his or her institution's collections and must exercise authority over their use regardless of patron invocations. The rare book librarian must judge the fragility of materials and act accordingly. While we do our best to provide access to materials, sometimes the condition of a book necessitates restricting its use.

User Documentation and Book Identification

The best policies on book handling will to a great extent prevent unintentional damage, but if there is a conscious effort to steal or damage materials, the act may be perpetrated and there must be a policy for events after the fact. Despite a high regard for the protection of invaluable materials, no one would advise actions that might endanger individuals. Anticipating potential danger, staff should have recourse to contact trained security personnel, and they should be advised to recognize and avoid imminent and potentially violent encounters. In most cases, however, missing or damaged materials may not be noted until some undetermined time after the fact. At such time, log-in records and visual records will demonstrate their usefulness as it provides law authorities with starting points for investigations.

In the past, there was reluctance by rare book libraries to publicize theft for fear that such incidents would reflect poorly upon the institution. Of late, however, the broadcasting of theft has been deemed more effective. First, widespread announcement of major theft alerts the rare book dealers who would be the common outlet for disposal of stolen goods. In fact, the Antiquarian Booksellers Association of America, the premier trade association of the rare book trade, designates a security officer for just such a purpose and this officer should be notified.[5] With this sort of transparency in mind, OCLC research created missingmaterials.org, a site where institutions can report missing materials and have them noted on the website, as well as in FirstSearch and WorldCat.org. Subscribers to the website receive notification of newly added materials via email or RSS feed.

The identification of stolen or lost books often depends on copy-specific bibliographic data. As noted in the discussion of bibliography, the importance of accurate descriptive records of library materials cannot be overemphasized. When a copy of the First Folio of Shakespeare's works (1623) mysteriously arrived at the Folger Shakespeare Library in the summer of 2008, it was identified as a copy stolen from Durham University ten years earlier. Although the book had been mutilated, copy-specific information such as the height and width of the text block, a manuscript annotation, typographical variants, and remnants of a stripped binding all helped prove beyond a doubt that the copy was indeed the Durham copy.[6] Similarly, in the Stephen Blumberg case, the Federal Bureau of Investigation, in co-operation with OCLC, utilized bibliographic data in order to identify books taken by Stephen Blumberg. A positive outcome of the Blumberg book thefts was the FBI's change of criteria for intervention in local theft cases. Previously, the FBI acted only in grand larceny cases that were interstate. That condition was emended to include any theft that exceeded $50,000, whether or not it was interstate or not, and prominent book thefts frequently meet these parameters.

Internal Theft

With regard to all the preventative measures that can be taken to deter theft and damage of library collections, the unfortunate fact persists that most library thefts are internal. In the case of the discovery of missing materials, suspicion by both institutional administrators and law officers will focus on rare book personnel, even the head of the rare book library. Under such circumstances, one can anticipate resentment and indignation from staff, and, in the vast majority of cases, such reactions are justified, for in most situations, the vast majority of rare book personnel are honest. Even with precautions, a rare book library cannot operate efficiently without a high degree of trust. In fact, from all our positive experiences with colleagues over the years, this entire issue is difficult, close to distasteful, to discuss, but because of historical circumstances, must be raised. On the brighter side, the general trustworthiness of the rare book community ensures that sound security measures, in balance with expected access to rare books in order for the library to function, will go a long way not only to protect the materials but also protect personnel from unwarranted allegations in the case of missing items. Rare book librarians must, however, steel themselves to the fact that there will be instances when books cannot be located.

Each institution should develop and implement its own internal security policies, which will vary according to the mission and activity of each individual library. Such policies should begin with the hiring process, as background checks of rare book personnel hires are highly recommended. Then there is the internal control of access to materials. Most obviously, the rarest and most valuable portions of the collections must be given the greatest security. Typically, such materials are housed in an extra-secure area within an already secure rare book stacks area, i.e., a vault within a vault. Again, the degree of security will vary: some institutions will have an actual vault, others may have a locked cage, or simply a separately locked room. Regardless of the level of secure housing, it is the level of access to that area that is critical. The fewer the number of people with access to the rarest materials—be it via key pad access or physical key—the greater the accountability, i.e., two people with access versus access by all staff. Even with access limited to a few people, separate sign-outs for keys can also be instituted so that there is a record of every entry to this inner sanctum (key pad access, of course, retains a constant record of access). Such monitoring of access will lead to a comprehensive record of evidence of entry to particularly important areas.

Another measure is the prohibition of any materials being kept at the desk or workstations of personnel unless the materials are being actively worked on. That is to say, all rare book materials are returned to the shelf, or, in some cases, a special holding area, at the end of the day. Also, the staff member should sign out for materials as if he or she was a general rare book patron. To emphasize and reiterate, this procedure ensures greater protection for the materials themselves, but also ensures personnel a measure of protection, should a particular item, which had been in the hands of a rare book employee, show up missing.

DISASTER PREPAREDNESS

Anticipation and accountability for security lapses of a human nature can lead to sound policies and procedures based on logic and experience. Natural disasters are another matter. They are frequently unanticipated, and institutional response must be immediate. Beyond natural disasters, there are failures of physical facilities systems as well, such as broken water mains

---

Recent Library Disasters

The history of library disasters extends from the ancient Library of Alexandria in 48 B.C. to the London conflagration of 1666 that destroyed numerous Shakespeare Third Folios to the burning of the Library of Congress in 1814. Such disasters continue today:

1966: Flood of the Arno River in Florence, Italy, which destroyed art, books, and manuscripts at the Uffizi Museum.

1986: A major fire destroyed 20 percent of the holdings of the Los Angeles Public Library on April 29. The cause was arson.

1998: Flood from heavy rains in an El Niño season flooded four libraries at Stanford University.

1998: In Boston, a burst water main, one of the city's oldest and largest, flooded the Boston Public Library shortly after midnight on a Sunday morning.

2007: In late fall, the Rare Book and Manuscript Library at the University of Illinois experienced a major mold outbreak.

---

and electrical fires. Whether a natural disaster or a mechanical failure, the institution can be proactive in its preparedness for response. First, there should be a well-defined order of communication, a priority of institutional contacts and disaster personnel, e.g., fire departments and security personnel, librarians supervisors, etc. An emergency telephone tree should exist for every special collections library, as it should for any professional organization. Professional emergency personnel, such as the fire department or emergency medical technicians, are trained in their responses. Local institutional personnel will require their own training and each institution should have a disaster preparedness team that meets on a regular basis to discuss responsibilities.

Emergency Planning

Water and fire are the greatest dangers to books and libraries and, in the case of fire, water inevitably follows. In cases of extreme water damage, there should be arrangements for rapid freezing of materials, and the disaster team should have a designated institutional freezer for just such situations. Freeze drying of paper prevents mold invasion since mold cannot grow at temperatures below about 65°F. Rapid freezing also prevents the smearing of ink.[7] At a college or university, food services are a logical location. Other facilities would include food warehouses and distribution centers. In the cases of lesser water damage, fans need to be close at hand so they can be blown on upright, splayed damp books.

Fire extinguishers should be at hand and all library personnel trained in their operation. Emergency kits should also be created and be comprehensive, accessible, and updated. They should be checked regularly to ensure completeness and operability.

Even though natural disasters are beyond human control, library personnel can anticipate the effects of extreme conditions and be particularly alert during such situations as hurricanes and subsequent floods; extreme cold and loss of power and broken water pipes; extreme heat; and failure of air conditioners and dehumidifiers. In a very real sense, then, system and mechanical failures are more unexpected than natural disasters in that there are no forewarnings—they may occur on a mild summer evening. The great flood at the Boston Public Library in 1998, for instance, was the result of a broken water main in the City of Boston's water system and was completely outside the control of the library.

Fire Extinguishing Systems

Rare book librarians must observe and monitor the institution's infrastructure as much as possible. To that extent, the rare book library should be equipped with preventative systems. In addition to emergency alarm systems wired to emergency personnel, the first line of defense might be a gas system that extinguishes fires by preventing further combustion in the rare book stacks. Libraries and museums frequently used Halon for this purpose, but it has been grandfathered out for environmental reasons and has in some cases been replaced with safer alternatives. Instead of, or in addition to, a gas-based suppressant, sprinklers or water mist systems are another line of defense, though a dry pipe system may be recommended. In this system there is no water in the sprinkler pipes until needed, thus preventing a pipe burst or leaking.

Unfortunately, not every institution is in a financial position to provide the latest in disaster preventative technology. Beyond such technological

---

Contents of an Emergency Kit

- A copy of your institution's disaster plan
- Plastic sheeting
- Scissors
- Plastic water buckets
- Sponges
- Flashlight and batteries
- Packages of freezer paper (for preparing items for cold storage)
- Hard hat
- Disposable clothing in small/medium/large
- Dust masks
- Paper towels
- Latex gloves in various sizes
- Cutter plus extra blades
- Extension cord
- Clean-up brushes

provisions, there are measures that rare book library personnel can undertake. Librarians are stewards of those materials under their care, but they are also the managers of the physical plant that houses those materials. Certainly, in every institution, there are maintenance personnel responsible for overseeing the care and upkeep of the physical buildings; yet maintenance departments can be woefully understaffed and overworked, thus undermining assiduous attention to their tasks. It is a sad statement that it is endemic to many institutions that the administration is eager and progressive in promoting and erecting new buildings, but passive and neglectful in the subsequent upkeep of those buildings. To that end, the rare book librarian should be an active participant in observing the condition of the physical library and alerting maintenance to actual and potential plant failures, for it is the home personnel of any building who are there day to day. Although a consistent maintenance schedule for such things as cleaning gutters and checking drains is the responsibility of the maintenance department, the library should work closely and cordially with that department to ensure timely inspections and operations and, perhaps, even establish a parallel maintenance schedule. Anticipation is the key to preparedness and, though no human being can account for every factor of existence, rare book librarians can look to the local and the obvious, for example, extreme weather conditions when the library is closed for an extended time, such as cold over the holidays or heat over the Fourth of July.

WHAT WILL SURVIVE: PRIORITIZING MATERIALS RESCUE

A final issue involves what materials in imminent danger can be saved and in what priority. Librarians and selected personnel need to know which items should be saved first in the case of disaster, should there be time to safely remove the items. Similarly, after the disaster event is over, librarians and selected personnel should know which items to salvage first in order to begin conservation treatment. Thus the disaster plan should indicate which items to save or salvage first. This can be presented in the form of a list of items and their locations, or perhaps a map with certain items indicated.

It must be stressed, in either the case of theft or disaster, personnel should never place themselves or others in any greater danger than they have to. Oftentimes life-threatening decisions must be made spontaneously, and as much anticipation, planning, and rehearsal that can precede such situations will benefit all.

THE IMPORTANCE OF SECURITY AND DISASTER PREPAREDNESS

Rare book librarians are charged with the care and protection of those books, manuscripts, and other materials that document our cultural history. Because libraries are often targets for thieves and occasionally the sites of natural disasters, librarians need to be prepared to handle such events. Emergency planning can limit overall damage to materials and ensure the safety and well-being of rare book personnel.

NOTES

1. As of the writing of this edition, we can point to recent major thefts: the Transylvania University thefts (2004) and the Forbes Smiley map thefts (2005). Unfortunately, should there be subsequent editions of this text, we will undoubtedly be able to cite yet ever more recent thefts.

2. See Nicholas A. Basbanes's *A Gentle Madness* (New York: Henry Holt and Company, 1995), for a thorough discussion of the Blumberg thefts.

3. This security practice is recommended in American Library Association Map and Geography Round Table. Map Collection Security Guidelines, revised by the MAGERT Task Force on Library Security for Cartographic Resources. Current guidelines (2010) posted at: http://www.ala.org/ala/mgrps/rts/magert/publicationsab/MAP%20COLLEC TION%20SECUR.pdf.

4. See Everett C. Wilkie, Jr., "Weighing Materials in Rare Book and Manuscript Libraries as a Security Measure against Theft and Vandalism," *RBM: A Journal of Rare Books, Manuscripts, and Cultural Heritage* 7, no. 2 (2006): 146–164.

5. In addition to the security arm of ABAA, the ACRL's "Guidelines for the Security of Rare Books, Manuscripts, and Other Special Collections" provide the names of other "Addresses for Reporting Thefts," such as the ACRL/RBMS Security Committee and the Society of American Archivists at http://www.ala.org/ala/mgrps/divs/acrl/standards/ securityrarebooks.cfm#ap3.

6. For a detailed description of the how the Durham First Folio was identified, see Richard Kuhta et al., "A Man Walks into a Library . . . The Curious Case of the Missing Durham First Folio," *Folger Magazine* 4, no. 3 (2010): 18–22, http://www.folger.edu/ library.cfm?libid=2888.

7. For further information about freeze drying and air drying, see "Drying Wet Books and Records," issued by the Northeast Documentation Center, at http://www.museum -security.org/drying-wet-books.html.

FURTHER READINGS

Fortson, Judith. *Disaster Planning and Recovery: A How-to-Do-It Manual for Librarians and Archivists*. New York: Neal-Schuman Publishers, 1992.

Kahn, Miriam. *The Library Security and Safety Guide to Prevention, Planning, and Response*. Chicago: American Library Association, 2008.

Lincoln, Alan Jan, and Carol Zall Lincoln. *Library Crime and Security: An International Perspective*. New York: Hawthorne Press, 1987.

RBMS Security Committee. "The Library and Archival Security Resources Directory," http://www.rbms.info/committees/security/security_resources .shtml. A comprehensive list of security resources.

Wellheiser, Johanna G., and Jude Scott. *An Ounce of Prevention: Integrated Disaster Planning for Archives, Libraries, and Record Centres*, 2nd ed. Lanham, MD: Scarecrow Press, 2002.

Wilkie, Everett C., Jr., ed. *Guide to Security Considerations and Practices for Rare Book, Manuscript, and Special Collection Libraries*. Chicago: Association of College and Research Libraries, 2011.

CHAPTER 7

Collection Development

Throughout this text we have and will continue to emphasize the importance of all aspects of rare book librarianship. But, if truth be known, collection development is perhaps the most important component of the rare book profession, for collections are, essentially, the raison d'être of libraries: without collections, there are no libraries. Analytical and descriptive bibliography may be the backbone of rare book librarianship, but if there are no books then there are no descriptions. Sound conservation and preservation programs may be essential to the enduring integrity of a rare book library, but if there are no collections then there are no books or manuscripts to preserve and secure. And so with all areas of rare book librarianship: public service, technical services, exhibitions, and donor relations.

Analogously, rare book librarians are not hired or appointed to positions unless there are collections to administer. There may be exceptional cases where someone is hired to build a collection to support a new academic program or research initiative, but even then there is a universe of extant materials that can be gathered to form the core of a new specialized library. Typically, in fact, when institutions advertise for a rare books or special collections librarian, the position will describe the content and extent of the collections that will be the responsibility of whomever assumes the position. That is to say, most rare book librarians, whether entering the field or moving to new positions, will have an established library to administer and to apply the other principles of rare book librarianship to ensure the growth, integrity, and use of the collections.

COLLECTION DEVELOPMENT POLICIES

A written collection development policy is an essential document for any rare book library. Such a policy is not typically detailed, but rather a general statement on the collecting goals and strategies for the rare book library. Most collection development policies usually provide information on how acquisitions support the library's mission, define the scope of the collection, identify the library's major collections, and list current collecting priorities. It would be surprising for any rare book librarian to find himself in a situation where some outline of collection goals, either tacit or formalized, was not in place. If such a plan is not in place, then one should be created immediately. If it is, then it should be reviewed and emended or updated on a periodical basis. The International Federation of Library Associations and Institutions outlines clearly the four principal reasons for creating a collection development policy in its "Guidelines for a Collection Development Policy Using the Conspectus Model" (2001).[1] The guidelines apply to all library collections, including rare book libraries. In brief, then:

(1)   Selection (a collection policy provides guidance to staff when selecting and deselecting resources for the collection);

(2)   Planning (it provides a sound foundation for future planning, thereby assisting in determining priorities, especially when financial sources are limited);

(3)   Public relations (it can be useful in making the case for the library when dealing with both its users, administrators, and funding bodies); and,

(4)   The wider context (it often serves as a basis for wider cooperation and resource sharing, whether in a locality, region, country, or even internationally).

Many institutions post their collection development policy on their websites, so there are a great many examples of good collection development policies online. Here are just a few:

• The Albert and Shirley Small Special Collections Library, University of Virginia:
  http://www2.lib.virginia.edu/small/collections/policy.html
• Fales Library, New York University Libraries:
  http://library.nyu.edu/collections/policies/fales.html
• James Madison University Libraries, Special Collections:
  http://www.lib.jmu.edu/faculty/specialcdpolicy.aspx

BUILDING UPON STRENGTH

Your collection development policy will define the library's strengths and, for many reasons, the truism of collection development is build upon strength. In the book's introduction, we argue that as the general collections of libraries grow increasingly singular, the rare and unique holdings will grow all the more special. If your rare book library boasts a strong collection on a certain topic, your library should strive to become a center for research on that topic; thus you will likely continue to build that collection. This is the idea of building on your strengths. Rare book libraries cannot realistically be comprehensive in the sense of developing rich research collections in all the areas of human knowledge. You might have a broad collection of selected materials for the purpose of teaching, but developing rich research collections that will satisfy scholars in every academic discipline is simply cost and space prohibitive. More likely, your collection development policy spells out areas of growth for your library, and these areas are where you put your resources. This doesn't rule out creating a new area of growth, which could be prompted by a shift in the focus of your local users. If, for example, your university hires a major James Joyce scholar, your library may want to acquire selected Joyce-related materials, recognizing of course that there are already major centers for Joyce studies and your mission is not to compete with them. But if your library received a major donation of Joyce materials, then you may indeed want to build actively on that collection. In this way, your library builds on the strength of its holdings but stays open to the prospect of growth for new areas of research.

Depending on your library's current strengths, you may be in the position to begin a new major collection. The Ohio State University's Rare Book and Manuscript Library, for example, recognized early the potential literary impact of author William T. Vollmann and began collecting his papers years before he won the National Book award in 2005 for *Europe Central*. The collection fits Ohio State's first-rate American fiction collection and serves as an example of acquiring archival materials for a modern author whose critical acclaim was still in its infancy. This requires staying on top of literary trends, plus a little prescience and luck. As an author's star rises, the cost of his or her archives rises, too.

The establishment of strong collections, which have been developed in concert with the interests and scholarship of an academic community or other constituency, has many ramifications. First, though research interests change, the general areas of excellence in a rare book library tend to remain stable, due in part to the reputation of its scholarly patrons or faculty (who in turn recruit graduate students), but also in part to the collections per se that have supported the research faculty over the generations. Second, suppliers of rare materials are familiar with collections and look toward specific institutions with known collection strengths when providing quotes and first refusal offers. Established collections will likely have in place a desiderata or want list, which facilitates the acquisition process. Third, friends of the rare book library, who know and have worked with the established collections, may have occasion to contribute, either in-kind or financially, to support collection development efforts. Such donors and friends may also refer others to the collection and promote the collection to a wider constituency beyond the institutional bounds. Fourth and finally, among other factors that can be considered, the known strength of a collection may attract donors who, though unaffiliated with the institution but with a keen interest in the research materials, may wish to place compatible collections in a library where they know the materials will be used and where the collections will continue to grow and prosper.

GLEANING FROM GENERAL COLLECTIONS

Important resources for the rare book library, especially one affiliated with a large academic or research library, are the general collections. Experienced rare book librarians have frequent occasion, when searching a bookseller catalog entry or a bookseller quote for duplicates, to discover that the book resides in the general collections. Unlike book collectors, who often place a higher premium on condition, rare book librarians often are more concerned with the subject content of a book, as opposed to its artifactual value, and an ex-libris copy of a desired title may be satisfactory, especially if the offered item would cost hundreds or even thousands of dollars. Large public or academic libraries of hundreds of thousands or millions of volumes will undoubtedly have important books that have languished in the general collections. Particularly, libraries that were founded and developed in the nineteenth and twentieth centuries will have books that were bought at the time of publication and have remained in the general collections. The 1999 *Preserving Research Collections: A Collaboration between Librarians and Scholars* (discussed in "A Brief History of Rare Book Libraries," Chapter 1) addressed the issue of treasures in the general collections, prompting a nationwide effort to take rare books out of circulation and transfer them into the secure environment of rare book libraries.[2]

ACQUISITION FUNDING AND COLLECTION ASSESSMENT

In Chapter 3, "Getting to Know Your Collections," we discuss the need to assess the origins and status of the artifacts in your rare book library. With regard to collection development, the rare book librarian needs to assess the origins and status of the funding support for the library:

- Are there institutional funds dedicated to the library as a whole and/or specific collections within?
- Are there endowments?
- Is there local or alumni support?
- Are there established exchange programs?

Having determined the extent of funding support, the rare book librarian should become familiar with the marketplace and fair market values for potential acquisitions in order to best expend whatever funds are available. Funding support varies greatly among institutions and determines significantly how funds are allocated and where collection development energies should be extended. We will discuss more about sources of materials, but highly funded rare book libraries are more likely to work with booksellers or auction houses whereas moderately or marginally funded libraries may choose to emphasize exchange programs or in-kind donations, though all libraries will ultimately utilize a variety of sources for resource development.

In a more general manner, there are present factors that you must weigh in your acquisitions decisions, such as: What is the current budget? What are your current collection needs? But there are future factors that you must always weigh: Will this item come on the market again? Will this item cost significantly more in the near future? Just as there are trends in art collecting, different genres of books have different values at different times. Books on cookery might be collectible at the moment, therefore increasing the amount you can expect to pay for a book on seventeenth-century cooking. Fishing seems to always be a hot topic. You must recognize that when trying to acquire an item, you are not just competing with other academic institutions, but also private book collectors. Still, as a caveat gleaned from experience, we refer you to John Carter's *Taste and Technique in Book Collecting* where he states "be less afraid of paying a stiff price than of letting slip some book you know to be rare and which is important to you. You cannot tell when, at what price, or even whether, you will see another."[3]

In truth, it is uncommon that rare book librarians on an annual or even decade basis can extensively develop all the collections under their aegis. In tandem with fund assessment, then, the rare book librarian should assess recent use of collections, specific acquisition requests, bequeathed collections, etc. To that end, in an academic or research library, recent scholarly use should be confirmed and, if possible, consult with the users of the collections: what are their research agendas, what do they foresee as new areas of research, are there new faculty whose research could be enhanced by focused acquisitions? With regard to endowed funds, are there family members or associates still actively supporting the fund? If so, such individuals should be contacted to ensure ongoing engagement with the collections.

In situations when collections have been promised to a library, the rare book librarian should meet with the donor and discuss expectations. In particular, this engagement will allow the library to plan for future purposes and work together in planning collection development. For instance, at Ohio State there is an impressive collection of eighteenth- and nineteenth-century British literature pledged to the library. The collection was developed by a faculty member who, though longtime tenured and financially comfortable, still would find it financially challenging to purchase the works of high point authors such as Jane Austen or William Blake. Ohio State was at one time, however, in a position to acquire four Austen items—*Mansfield Park*, *Emma*, and *Northanger Abbey* and *Persuasion*, two titles published together—and, by doing so, not only pleased the donor but also enriched its own collections in light of what would come to the institution at the present time. On the other hand, by working with the donor and becoming familiar with his personal library, Ohio State can defer on much eighteenth- and nineteenth-century British literature with the certainty that the titles will eventually be part of the permanent collections. Those funds that might have been used, then, can be applied to other areas of collection development.

The rare book librarian must bear in mind, however, that no library can collect everything in the sense that the collection will have the breadth and depth necessary to define it as a research resource. Unwanted gifts are discussed further in the "Working with Donors" section of Chapter Ten, part 1, but we note briefly here that one of the more difficult situations for a rare book librarian is turning away potential gifts that are offered with the best of intentions: feelings may be hurt and future fruitful relations jeopardized. Having noted this particular predicament, each case will have different ramifications that may dictate the final disposition of any proffered collection. Tact and honesty with regard to the collection will always remain the best policy. Again, the collection development policy will prove useful in guiding forays into possibly ill judged or misguided acquisitions. This is not to say that the library would reject exempla of types of materials for the purpose of teaching or demonstration, such as medieval manuscripts, incunabula, or musical scores, but to accept everything, even as gifts, incurs expense. Nothing is ever really free, and processing and storage costs directed to inconsequential collections diverts funds that could be better applied for providing access to collections of distinction. Nor is this to discourage exploration of adding new collections of exceptional strength (after all, most great collections were developed from strong core collections given en bloc to institutions), but to weigh the advantages and disadvantages in light of current collection strengths, constituency research interests, and ability to develop the collections further.

THE MARKETPLACE AND THE BOOK TRADE

With collection assessment in place and content priorities established, strategies for acquisition can be implemented. It would be no surprise that most current and prospective rare book librarians are denizens of bookstores and a prerogative of any rare book librarian is to simply search for books independently. And, though such an individual approach will be practiced by most rare book librarians (with cautions that will be discussed under ethical concerns), there are distinct inefficiencies in such an approach to book acquisition, not the least being that it is labor intensive and thus weakens efforts in the many other areas of responsibility that fall upon the rare book librarian's shoulders.

The single most important source of materials for the rare book library is booksellers. The rare book trade has an honored and illustrious history and remains firmly established, though physical bookstores are rapidly becoming virtual bookstores on the Internet. Still, what has always determined the success of sellers of rare books is the stock on hand, and that criterion continues to this day. Booksellers are devoted full time to their trade, know better than anyone else the source for rare and special books, and cultivate a vast network of other professionals. Moreover, though we would hope that all book collectors would approach libraries first, in fact, most collectors or heirs of collectors are looking first for remuneration rather than institutional recognition. In particular, just as with rare book libraries, many distinguished rare booksellers have distinct specialties—e.g., history of science, law, medieval manuscripts—and are natural outlets for collectors in those areas. In fact, private collectors may well have longtime relations with a particular dealer, and it is natural to go to that source when contemplating the disposition of a library.

Every rare book librarian will initiate and nurture business relations with a network of booksellers that will vary in size based on the extent of the institution's rare book holdings, collecting priorities that may alter over time or even from year to year, and funding support. We would stress that the network of booksellers be selective in order that the librarian and the bookseller can maintain close communication with regard to collection development goals. Too wide a network could vitiate energy and even create an artificial competition if the situation exists that too many booksellers are looking for the same books. Although the rare book market is large and diverse, within areas of specialization the market can actually be quite small. If a focused collection has a lacuna, then that gap alone is indicative of the scarcity of the desired book. After all, most rare book collections have been developed over many years, and if a prominent item is still lacking, then it must, indeed, be exceedingly rare. In that case, if several booksellers are looking for what may be a unique item on the current book market, they will be bidding against each other to acquire it and hence raise the value. Even in the case where desired books may exist in greater numbers on the market, competing booksellers are buying the same item with a particular rare book library in mind, but only one will make a sale. Though the other booksellers will undoubtedly find a buyer at some point in time, the expectation was that a sale was imminent and, if too many sales are rejected, it could discourage further attentiveness to your needs and corrode your relationship with a particular bookseller.

A desiderata list, i.e., a wish list, is a useful resource to develop in order to distribute to booksellers, with the admonition just noted above, that the book market should not be flooded with such lists. This is not to say that a bookseller expects that every offer will result in a sale, but that the bookseller should expect a reasonably high return on books acquired from a desiderata list. When working from a desiderata list, booksellers will quote items to libraries, that is, they offer the library first refusal, a considerable benefit in the competitive rare book market.

Beyond soliciting the services of booksellers, a desiderata list is an important tool for the rare book librarian as well. First, though the rare book librarian may choose to work with a network of booksellers, that decision does not preclude the fact that rare book librarians themselves will remain attentive to the book market and the rare book collection needs. The rare book librarian should never cede collection development responsibilities solely to booksellers who are agents for the library. It would be an odd rare book librarian, indeed, who did not have an enthusiasm for books and collections and the desire to be active in the collection development process. Hundreds of rare book catalogs and lists, in print or electronically transmitted, will pass through the rare book library annually and the rare book librarian will identify many items for purchase. Awareness of needs, as reinforced by frequent reference to the desiderata list, will expedite response to catalogs.

Just as there is competition among booksellers, there is competition among rare book libraries that collect in similar areas. As noted, booksellers can provide the useful service of first refusal, but when an item appears in a catalog it is available for the rare book market at large. To ensure acquisition, prompt perusal and response to catalog entries is mandatory because desired books sell fast and a rare book librarian needs to contact the bookseller for confirmation as soon as possible. For instance, the William Charvat Collection of American Fiction at Ohio State is an extremely strong collection, particularly for fiction in the twentieth century. Yet, for all its strength, the collection was lacking a copy of *Cane*, Jean Toomer's 1923 classic work from the Harlem Renaissance. When it appeared in a dealer's catalog, a confirmation call was made only to discover that this copy of *Cane* had sold but five minutes earlier. To emphasize, he who hesitates is lost and the annals of rare book librarianship are replete with tales of similar disappointments.

Rare book librarians need not be reactive only but should take a proactive role in collection development as well. Certainly, even in close working relations with booksellers, it is the rare book librarian who knows the collection best and, in the age of electronic resources, there are expanded capabilities to identify desired books and materials through such rare book search engines as viaLibri.net, ABE.com, and Alibris.com. The caution here is that not all inventories are up to date and not all booksellers are as accurate in their bibliographic descriptions as are booksellers affiliated with the professional book associations. A morning of searching could yield disappointing results, though, on the other hand, it could also yield unexpected surprises.

Although we emphasize that the ultimate responsibility for collection development resides with the rare book librarian, booksellers and the book trade marketplace almost inevitably will be part of the process. In particular, we wish to note two particular roles of booksellers that can prove invaluable: as representatives of a service industry and as intermediaries with private collectors. With knowledge of a rare book library's collections and needs, booksellers, through their wide, special, and secretive sources (booksellers are protective of their contacts), will have access to multitudes of unrecorded books. They can find many rare books prior to their appearance on the book market and, if they identify items that a rare book library is looking for, can quote them directly before adding them to open stock or listing them in a catalog. In other cases, the rare book librarian may prevail upon certain booksellers to send early proofs of catalogs that address collections needs. Advanced proofs from booksellers overseas are of especial importance in the United States. So too, many booksellers have a network of book scouts who scour the countryside—antique stores, thrift shops, library sales, garage sales, etc.—and are attentive to those specialized books that might seem insignificant to the casual browser but catch the eye of the informed and astute book scout. For instance, the late Peter Howard of Serendipity Books of Berkeley, California, claimed to have the "best damned scouts in the west," and over the years his scouts identified and secured thousands of books for the William Charvat Collection of American Fiction at Ohio State, fiction published by small presses, local imprints, limited copies, or self-published works of little-known authors who are often overlooked by book buyers who are hunting for the Hemingways and Steinbecks. Also it is not uncommon that a bookseller will offer to a rare book library a title that is not on any desiderata list primarily because it was previously not known to exist. Common, too, is the statement that "you don't know this, but you want this book," and, often, that statement proves true.

There are occasions when a rare book library may have the opportunity to acquire a private library or a literary archive of a prominent writer. Although the rare book librarian may be perfectly capable of negotiating the acquisition (and many rare book librarians do), such purchases, not donations, do involve money, and financial dealings can affect other relations in a negative way if a subsequent sense of unfairness impugns the efforts of the rare book library. Let us emphasize that many direct acquisitions do proceed amicably, but one should be advised that a short-term advantage may have long-term recriminations. Booksellers can play a useful role as intermediaries in that they serve as agent and advocate for the selling party. The intermediary role, involving finances, can relieve the rare book librarian of a perceived procurer role and allow the rare book librarian and owner to deal with curatorial issues such as plans for further development of the collection, promotion of the collection, and, perhaps, future tangible commitments from the owner. The bookselling trade is a service industry and the commission involved in a single transaction may be more than repaid by long-term commitments and loyalties of a satisfied customer.

AUCTIONS

Book auctions have been an integral component of the rare book market for centuries. If possible the rare book library should be on the mailing list of prominent auction houses such as Bonhams, Christie's, Sotheby's, and Swann. As in the art world, book auctions are a determining factor in current values, and the catalogs, with their detailed bibliographic description and provenance notes, are important reference sources in addition to their importance to the acquisition process. Book auctions most commonly are the sale of distinguished private collections often compiled with a distinct intellectual design and decided content focus. Frequently, books of extreme rarity show up at auction, and the books tend to be in very good condition. As opposed to ordering at set cost from a bookseller's catalog or responding to a quote, auctions are an open market and the values may exceed considerably the estimates in the catalog. Also, sales at auction often include a buyer's premium, a percentage fee assessed to the purchase and added to the winning bid. (Percentages differ among auction houses and can be ascertained from the auction house itself.)

Anyone can attend an auction and participate directly, though it is expensive and time consuming for a rare book librarian to attend auctions, which most often occur in major cities such as London or New York. Moreover, there are protocols and skills associated with the competitive auction that may work to the disadvantage of those rare book librarians who are inexperienced with the real-time auction activity, as we suspect most are. Exigencies do exist, however, that enable participation of a rare book library in the auction process. First, the rare book librarian can submit a maximum bid prior to the auction. That will involve ascertaining the estimates from the auction catalog and then assessing library funds and how much above the high estimate the library is willing to go without forgetting to add in the buyer's premium. The auction house itself then will bid for the client. Secondly, every auction house has staff that will bid for the library, typically via a telephone connection. In the case of intermediary bidding, a maximum bid need not be submitted prior to the auction. Rather, the rare book librarian will be connected to an auction house staff member who will bid for the library as directed. As a note of caution, based on experience, auction bidding proceeds at a rapid rate: hundreds of lots will go under the hammer during a typical six-hour session. There is no dawdling during an auction and indecision is fatal, for he who hesitates at auction will surely lose. It is difficult enough to respond in a timely manner while actually present at the auction and even the slight delay intrinsic to telephone bidding can lose a lot, for, when the hammer falls, there is no reopening of the bid. In fact, when the bid is conferred by the auction staff to the librarian, there is but time to say yes or no. For instance, Ohio State had a distinct interest in a William S. Burroughs notebook at auction in Sotheby's Allen Ginsberg sale in 1999. Bidding was done with a Sotheby's staff member and, as described above, the proceedings were rapid and the bid reached Ohio State's allocated committed fund in short fashion. This was not a mailed bid, however, and Sotheby's was unaware of Ohio State's commitment. The next-level bid was provided and, without hesitancy, Ohio State said yes, exceeding the committed fund: that final bid held. Obviously, the rare book librarian felt confidence with asserting some latitude—with good fortune in this case—but too much liberality might have incurred some disapproval from library administration. Many factors were at play during this transaction that took less than five minutes: there was scant time for rumination, and intuition prevailed.

THE IMPORTANCE OF COLLECTION DEVELOPMENT

In recapitulation and summary, collection development is the most important responsibility of the rare book librarian for it generates all the other responsibilities and tasks related to rare book librarianship. As we hope we have shown, the means and wherefores for developing collections are vast and diverse, and the rare book librarian will devise numerous strategies and develop many relationships to ensure the consistent and fruitful growth of the collections. On a personal level, the development of great collections can be the single most lasting imprint of the rare book librarian. Establishing extensive and coherent research resources that will endure for generations of scholars is a time-honored legacy and profound contribution to the annals of collected knowledge.

NOTES

1. See http://archive.ifla.org/VII/s14/nd1/gcdp-e.pdf.

2. See http://www.mla.org/rep_preserving_collections. A subsequent article, "Guidelines on the Selection and Transfer of Materials from General Collections to Special Collections," issued by an ACRL Rare Books and Manuscripts Section Task Force, (*College and Research Libraries News* 69, no. 10 (November 2008): 630–637,) further clarifies "guidelines on the selection and transfer of materials from General Collection to Special Collections divisions" including "transfer policy, shelving, preservation assessment, cataloging, market value, and the bibliographic and research value" of materials.

3. John Carter, *Taste and Technique in Book Collecting* (Cambridge: Cambridge University Press, 1948. Rpt. London: Private Libraries Association, 1970), 136.

FURTHER READINGS

Anderson, Joanne S. ed. *Guide for Written Collection Policy Statements* (Chicago: ALA Editions, 1996).

Guide for Written Collection Policy Statements. Subcommittee to Revise the Guide for Written Collecting Policy Statements, Administration of Collection Development Committee, Collection Management and Development Section, ed. Chicago: American Library Association, 1996.

"Guidelines on the Selection and Transfer of Materials from General Collections to Special Collections." *Association of College and Research Libraries: A Division of the American Library Association.* 1 July 2008. http://www.ala.org/ala/mgrps/divs/acrl/standards/selctransfer.cfm.

Gwinn, Nancy E., and Paul H. Mosher. "Coordinating Collection Development: The RLG Conspectus." *College & Research Libraries* 44, no. 2 (March 1983): 128–140.

"Resources for Library Collections." Association for Library Collections & Technical Services. http://www.ala.org/alcts/resources/collect

CHAPTER 8

Accessioning and Cataloging

In briefest terms, the mission of all libraries, rare book libraries included, is preservation and access: identifying, securing, and conserving the universe of knowledge and, subsequently, providing users with the means to engage with those materials. This chapter focuses on accessioning and cataloging, the essential functions through which rare books are identified, organized, and made accessible to library users.

IDENTIFICATION AND DESCRIPTION OF NEW ACQUISITIONS

Trained in bibliographic description, the rare book librarian has a primary responsibility, upon receipt of new acquisitions, to ensure that the books received are what they were reputed to be by the dealer or donor. This is not to suggest any conscious misrepresentations by book dealers, but rather to view the reality that there are different levels of competencies and attention to detail in all professions: even the most trusted and reliable of dealers may err on occasion. The first step in identification is to collate the book or, for modern books, confirm pagination. As Roderick Cave notes:

> In collating the material, the librarian's basic task is to see that it corresponds with the description of the item in the auction or bookseller's catalogue from which it was ordered. A secondary, but no less important, duty is to check with bibliographies and other appropriate authorities to see that the book matches up to the descriptions there.[1]

COPY-SPECIFIC DESCRIPTION

In most instances, authoritative bibliographies provide ideal descriptions of books from specific printings although there could be many variants among the copies printed, especially with early books when press runs were interrupted to correct errors. Also, any given book after printing will incur additions and excisions due to use and reading habits. The concept of the copy-specific book, then, is integral to all discussion of rare books and will be used commonly in the discussion of accessioning and cataloging. A copy-specific book is a single identified book or other printed matter, not simply any copy of print run or published edition. Although the ideal description of the book is useful for general confirmation of its authenticity, the book should also be examined for copy-specific information that differentiates it from other like items. The Center for Bibliographic Studies and Research at the University of California at Riverside provides guidelines for recording copy-specific and provenance notes in its English Short Title Catalog (ESTC).[2] ESTC prescribes documentation for "Non-negative physical characteristics" (what *is there*, in the book, such as variants, manuscript notes, author's presentation copy, binder's ticket, etc.) as opposed to "Imperfections" (what *should be there* in the book but is not, such as lacking leaves; other subsequent treatment of the book, such as mutilations and repairs; and miscellaneous observations, such as lightly printed pages or leaves from another copy).

Ultimately, every book is unique because of its copy-specific characteristics, such as bindings, page tears, water stains, and owner markings. In addition to the copy-specific information that may prove useful to researchers, it is essential to record copy-specific details for security reasons. Time may pass before the book is fully cataloged and the more detail provided in a catalog record, the more evidence you have to help identify a book should it be stolen. In the meantime, you should have a system that records distinguishing features found in the book. This may include taking digital photographs of at-risk materials such as maps. The British Library's Vulnerable Collection Items Project provides a good working model for this identification process.[3]

As a final step in inspecting new rare book acquisitions, examine the condition of the book and if necessary write up a conservation report. If possible this should be a page-by-page review. Use an attention flag to point out loose material, detached boards, torn pages, and other flaws. If the item is unstable in its current condition, consider sending it immediately for conservation treatment, or rehouse the book in a manner that stabilizes the book until it can be treated. In addition to addressing the physical integrity of individual books, be aware that a book can potentially damage the books around it. For example, red rot, acidic leather dust from a book's binding, could migrate to the bindings around it; or metal bosses (raised metal ornamentation) on a binding could dig into surrounding books. These books should be housed in phase boxes or clamshell boxes as a preventive measure. In the case of a large book with metal bosses, you may want to store that book horizontally (as it was likely originally designed to be shelved).

CATALOGING PRIORITIES AND PROCEDURES

Having urged the rare book librarian to be as conscientious as possible in identification of individual books and other materials, it must be said that we are idealizing the descriptive process. Beyond the rare book librarian's inspection, few libraries will have the qualified staff to devote to the assiduous process of rare book cataloging, and, hence, the amount of description will be determined by the curatorial decision as to which books are of the highest priority. Still, even if a rare book librarian cannot meet the ideal of descriptive cataloging, rare books do require more than minimal cataloging. Users of general collections most often seek content and information only and any text or derivative will do. For instance, a student may wish to read Samuel Taylor Coleridge's "The Rime of the Ancient Mariner," and though the 1798 edition of *Lyrical Ballads* would meet the need, the student would likely be satisfied with a modern edition, a photocopy, or an electronic version. Many users of rare book libraries, however, are often seeking specific editions or printings. They may also be consulting not just a particular edition, but a specific copy based on provenance, marks in the books, or original bindings. This is not to say that cataloging of general collections should receive anything but accurate and reliable description, but rather to suggest that rare and special materials should receive greater detail in order to meet the heightened research demands of their scholarly community.

This assertion is attested to by the Rare Books and Manuscripts Section (RBMS) of the Association of College and Research Libraries of the American Library Association whose Bibliographic Standards Committee has, over a great number of years, created and distributed its *Descriptive Cataloging of Rare Materials* for books, manuscripts, serials, and other materials.[4] Among its many charges is "the establishment of bibliographic standards whereby the unique requirements of special collections may be addressed; to disseminate information pertinent to librarians and others responsible for providing intellectual access to special collections." Here are links to few strong examples of rare book cataloging:

Brigham Young University: http://catalog.lib.byu.edu/uhtbin/pcnum/ 4928787
Folger Shakespeare Library: http://shakespeare.folger.edu/cgi-bin/ Pwebrecon.cgi?BBID=166785
University of California, Berkeley: http://oskicat.berkeley.edu/ record=b10997375~S1

Most rare book librarians, in light of other principal responsibilities (collection development, public service, promotion and publicity, donor relations), will not have the time to catalog rare book materials and will rely upon and work closely with cataloging staff. This does not abrogate the rare book librarian from the accessioning process, as described above, nor from ensuring that rare book cataloging standards are maintained. Rare book cataloging is a field unto itself, and it is imperative for the rare book librarian to be engaged with it. This includes knowing current practices and standards, so that you may work closely and collaboratively with catalogers. Major rare book and special collection libraries will likely have catalogers assigned to rare and special materials. Yet each individual library will have cataloging policies and procedures in place and, in fact, the rare book librarian, in some cases, may be limited in the level of cataloging detail that can be expected. That being the case, the rare book librarian should, none the less, strive for the most complete rare book cataloging and, in some cases, augment or enhance catalog records with other data, such as additional bibliographic or provenance information that can be supplied to cataloging staff.

NONPRINT COLLECTIONS

A particular processing challenge for a rare book librarian is large collections of nonbook materials—literary archives or historical documents—that arrive en bloc in dozens, scores, or hundreds of containers. Such collections typically fall outside the purview of normal cataloging workflows. Certainly, upon receipt, a collection-level record can and should be created that describes the extent of the collection, e.g., number of boxes, linear feet or cubic feet, so that potential users will learn of its existence and, in the case of a vast collection, realize that detailed information regarding the collection contents may not be immediate. In fact, a note should be made as to the status of the collection's processing. A collection-level record, however, need not be absolutely minimal. In notes sections, a collection narrative can offer extensive descriptive information about the contents and formats of the collection including such areas as manuscripts, correspondence, photographs, etc., inclusive dates of the materials, provenance, and more. Added entries can identify salient contributors to the archive. In modern online public access catalogs these notes and added entries will become access points. In the long run, due to the extent and detail of large nonbook collections, catalog records for individual items will not be created. Rather, rare book library staff will create a finding aid that can provide access to the box level, folder level, or, with exceptional collections, the item level. The finding aid can be linked to the collection-level catalog record and fulfill the access needs for the user. Here is a link to a find aiding from The Ohio State University for

the archive of the artist Lillian Schwartz: http://library.osu.edu/find/collec
tions/rarebooks/RBMScollections/lillian-schwartz/.

In recent years, the special collections and archives communities have
addressed the need to reassess manuscript processing especially in light of
the mass of paper collections that are inundating virtually all major research
repositories. In the oft-cited "More Product, Less Process: Revamping
Traditional Archival Processing," Mark A. Greene and Dennis Meissner
note that "processing backlogs continue to be a problem for archivists and
yet the problem is exacerbated by many of the traditional approaches to
processing collections that archivists continue to practice." Supported by a
thorough examination of the literature on archival processing and supported by an extensive survey of the professional field, the authors issue "a
call for archivists to rethink the way they process collections, particularly
contemporary collections" wherein they challenge "many of the assump-
tions archivists make about the importance of preservation and the arrangement and description activities necessary to allow researchers to access
collections effectively."[5] Your institution undoubtedly has processing policies in place and processing priorities set. If, however, your institution has
significant processing backlogs, as Greene and Meissner's national survey
documents that the majority of major archival repositories do, then a reexamination of current processing policies might well be worth undertaking
in order to expedite access to your processing backlog. To that end, an
important first step would be to create a list of unprocessed or minimally
processed collections that would be available to the research community:
even a single line title of a collection is better than no record at all.

CATALOGING AND PROFESSIONAL ETHICS

Cataloging and processing are essential, and rare book librarians, as well
as archivists and other stewards of research materials, are both professionally and ethically bound to make the contents of their collections known.
The RBMS Code of Ethics states that "the library's rules for access and use
must be applied and enforced equally, according to the terms of the ALA/
SAA *Joint Statement on Access to Original Research Materials*."[6] The Joint
Statement, in addition to the Code of Ethics and numerous other professional documents, is extensive and should be consulted on a regular basis.
According to the statement:

As the accessibility of material depends on knowing of its existence, it
is the repository's responsibility to inform researchers of the collections in its custody. This may be accomplished through local, regional,
or national catalogs; inventories and other internal finding aids; published guides; and the assistance of staff members.

THE IMPORTANCE OF ACCESSIONING AND CATALOGING

The purpose of accessioning and cataloging is to provide, in a timely manner, accurate and, to the extent possible, detailed records of new acquisitions of the rare book library. Expeditious processing will generate confidence among researchers and endear donors. We must conclude with the stark reality that, due to fiscal exigencies, there are book backlogs and languishing collections in rare book libraries everywhere. Such situations should be minimized as much as possible, for poor access could adversely affect a library's reputation in that patrons could lose confidence and donors become disillusioned. Having said that, rare book librarians should strive to promote processing to the greatest extent of their influence, both for the immediate access to the collection and also for their constituency's long-term commitment to collection development goals.

NOTES

1. Roderick Cave, *Rare Book Librarianship*, rev. ed. (London: C. Bingley, 1982), 65.
2. See http://estc.ucr.edu/starhelp/copy_notes.html.
3. See Kimberly C. Kowal and John Rhatigan, "The British Library's Vulnerable Collection Items Project," *Liber Quarterly* 18, no. 2 (2008): 76–79, online at http://liber.library.uu.nl/publish/articles/000247/article.pdf.
4. See http://www.rbms.info/committees/bibliographic_standards/dcrm/dcrmtext.html.
5. Mark A. Greene and Dennis Meissner, "More Product, Less Process: Revamping Traditional Archival Processing," *American Archivist* 68, no. 2 (Fall/Winter 2005): 208–263.
6. See http://www.archivists.org/statements/alasaa.asp.

FURTHER READINGS

Descriptive Cataloging of Rare Materials (Books). Washington, DC: Library of Congress Cataloging Distribution Service, 2008. [Additional guides are available for descriptive cataloging of serials, music, graphics, manuscripts and cartographic materials.]

O'Toole, James M. *Understanding Archives and Manuscripts*. Chicago: Society of American Archivists, 1990.

Russell, Beth M. "Description and Access in Rare Books Cataloging: A Historical Survey." *Cataloging & Classification Quarterly* 35, no. 3–4 (2003): 491–523.

Stalker, Laura, and Jackie M. Dooley. "Descriptive Cataloging and Rare Rooks." *Rare Books and Manuscripts Librarianship* 7, no. 1 (1992): 7–23.

CHAPTER 9

Copyright

Copyright is the legal ownership of creative works, be they text, image, music, software, etc. Copyright protects the rights of the creator for all profit derived from original work and prohibits the unwarranted use of the original work by other parties. Although simple in concept, copyright is complex in application and verification. The fact that an extensive number of copyright cases have reached the Supreme Court of the United States attests to the intricacies of the U.S. Copyright Act.[1] Current copyright law states that copyright belongs to the creator, the creator's heirs or other assignee for seventy years after the death of the creator, generally, though other restrictions can be applied. This criterion applies only to those writers, artists, composers, etc., who died after 1950, a stipulation that will become increasingly moot over time. The history of copyright is fascinating and of great usefulness in certain bibliographic research, but for current rare book librarians, familiarity with contemporary copyright law is most essential. For help in determining the copyright status of a work, see Peter Hirtle's extremely useful chart "Copyright Term and the Public Domain in the United States," http://www.copyright.cornell.edu/resources/publicdomain.cfm.[2]

PHYSICAL PROPERTY, INTELLECTUAL PROPERTY, AND PUBLIC DOMAIN

The most important factor regarding library property and copyright is the distinction between the physical property and the intellectual property. Collections owned by a library are the physical property of that library and can be administered with regard to access and preservation in accord with the good stewardship expected of a responsible library. Dependent upon conditions associated with any library collection (e.g., restricted access placed on donated collections), the library has the right to provide access to the physical property. The intellectual property, however, remains with the creator, the creator's heirs, or other assigned copyright holder. In some cases, the library or other holding institution may, in fact, become the copyright holder. If a patron wishes to reproduce materials, in whatever format, the patron must have written permission from the copyright holder. This same provision applies to the institution as well, i.e., the rare book library cannot reproduce materials without permission of the copyright holder.

The good news for most rare book librarians is that many of their collections are in the public domain. Currently, works published before 1923 are in the public domain. Since a great mass of rare materials precedes that date these works can be reproduced with impunity. For instance, the digitization of an early collection (Shakespeare, Cervantes, or Melville) can be made publically accessible to the worldwide scholarly community without threat of violating copyright law. Still, rare book and special collections libraries contain a wealth of holdings created after 1923, both published and unpublished materials, that fall under copyright law, and prudence must be practiced in reproducing these materials. As digitization of printed, visual, and audio works continues to proliferate, with extensive materials coming from libraries (frequently from rare and special collections), particular attention must be paid to copyright ownership.

Though digitization and its rapid, international access can be the more conspicuous and far-reaching form of copyright infringement, the rare book librarian must remember that even the casual photocopying of a single manuscript leaf for a supporting faculty member or loyal patron can also violate copyright, because copyright violation is not a matter of extent or degree, but absolute: either the text or image is or is not under copyright, and if it is under copyright, either an institution has permission or does not have permission from the copyright holder to reproduce the text or image.

In the practical world, we acknowledge that copyright law is violated on a frequent basis. Public photocopy machines, present in every library, display the obligatory notice that photocopying of current materials may be in violation of copyright. Yet, we all know that library patrons ignore this provision and violate copyright on a daily basis. The difference in rare book libraries is that the librarians usually make photocopies for their patrons, which may make them complicit in violation of copyright law. In light of rampant copyright violation in public sectors, the refusal of a rare book librarian to make photocopies for patrons when copyright clearance is in doubt can result in strained patron relations. Further explanation follows with regard to unpublished materials, where restraints are more clear though more severe, and published materials, where the fair use provision applies.

FAIR USE

Fair use, as with copyright law generally, seems a simple concept, but it is really a gray area subject to multiple interpretations. Under Section 107 of U.S. Copyright Law, limitations on copyright are noted (e.g., teaching, scholarship, criticism, etc.) and four factors for determining fair use are provided:

- the purpose and character of use, nonprofit, educational use weighing in favor of fair use vs. commercial use;
- the nature of the work, nonfiction and published works weighing in favor of fair use versus fiction and unpublished works;
- the amount of material used relative to the total work with the least amount weighing in favor of fair use; and,
- the market of the work, classroom use, for instance, weighing on the side of fair use versus a course packet.

Fortunately, fair-use provisions are widely documented, as are useful charts of positive and negative applications that can guide the rare book librarian in this process. All provisions of copyright law, including Fair Use, are accessible through the U.S. Copyright Office, but numerous documents are long and detailed.[3] A rare book library, therefore, should have readily available a checklist of fair-use provisions that will resolve the majority of cases. Columbia University's Copyright Advisory Office, for instance, has a helpful checklist at http://copyright.columbia.edu/copyright/files/2009/10/fairusechecklist.pdf. In addition, many research institutions will have a copyright office that can be consulted in more difficult cases.

Since any material published after 1923 can be under copyright, care must be taken to confirm copyright ownership. Many research libraries have extensive holdings of twentieth- and twenty-first-century materials, and due diligence should be taken to document copyright holders of such materials. As a collection is acquired, copyright holders should be made part of the permanent record for that collection and updated over time. Certainly, if a collection of a personal author or corporate body is acquired directly, copyright will be known at that time; but, if copyright ownership is in any doubt, that fact should be clarified as soon as possible and made a part of the permanent record. For published materials, copyright can be ascertained through a search of the Copyright Division of the Library of Congress, but be advised that such a search can be very expensive. For unpublished materials, other sources must be consulted. One such source is Writers, Artists and Their Copyright Holders (WATCH), a joint venture of Harry Ransom Center at the University of Texas and the University of Reading in England.[4] As a word of a caution, it must be noted that there can be competing copyright claims that can only be determined by a court of law.

UNPUBLISHED WORKS

Copyright law is more restrictive toward unpublished works for a very simple reason: the creator has yet to profit from unpublished works, thus, obviously, increasing the potential earning value of those works. The severer restrictions for unpublished materials is of utmost importance since most research libraries distinguish themselves with unique collections of literary and historical archives that may contain an abundance of such material, particularly correspondence, and are especially alluring to scholars. The more stringent provision was clarified in a monumental copyright case, *J. D. Salinger vs. Random House and Ian Hamilton.* Ian Hamilton, a noted biographer, was writing the life story of the renowned and very private author J. D. Salinger. As with any good researcher, Hamilton had recourse to examine Salinger's papers and correspondence at various research libraries. When it came time to publish the biography, Salinger, who had received advanced proofs of the book, took suit against Hamilton's publisher, Random House, exerting his copyright ownership and refusing permission for Hamilton to quote or even paraphrase from his personal letters, a restriction that would essentially scuttle publication of the biography. In 1987, the U.S. Court of Appeals for the Second Circuit concurred with Salinger and ruled that Hamilton could not quote or paraphrase from his letters. Despite defense arguments about fair use, the court was adamant in its ruling that Hamilton could report only facts. The U.S. Supreme Court refused to review the Court of Appeals ruling.[5] Three years later (1990), the Supreme Court remained consistent and refused the appeal of Henry Holt Co. (*New Era Publications International, Aps v. Henry Holt and Co.,* 873, F.2d 576 [2nd Cir 1989]) to quote from the unpublished writings of Scientology founder L. Ron Hubbard in Russell Miller's unauthorized biography, *Bare-Faced Messiah.*

Fair-use proponents assailed these court rulings because they dramatically limited the use of original materials, which have been and remain the stalwarts of scholarly publishing, particularly for later twentieth- and early twenty-first-century research. The restriction of even paraphrasing from copyrighted, unpublished papers was particularly egregious for scholars who, in the past, had frequent and extensive recourse to paraphrase with impunity. At the time of the Salinger decision, Robert A. Gorman noted:

> The fair use doctrine was explicitly incorporated in statutory law for the first time in the 1978 Copyright Act. Section 107 includes among illustrative examples of fair use "criticism, comment, news reporting, teaching (including multiple copies for classroom use), scholarship or research." These are not automatically immune from copyright liability; they are simply to be viewed with special kindness.[6]

Despite increased restrictions regarding publication of previously unpublished materials, fair use still has legal currency, though more specifically for citations from printed works. Still, though fair use applications can be defined, the extent of quotation remains undefined, and as Gorman notes, such applications are "viewed with special kindness" and not necessarily guaranteed. To that end, then, the librarian must be prudent as to not only *what* but also to *what extent* materials under copyright may be reproduced.

ORPHAN WORKS

Orphan works, where the copyright holder cannot be determined, pose a particular challenge for rare book librarians. Literally millions of such works, such as photographs, audio and video recordings, letters, diaries, and more, exist in libraries throughout the nation. Although libraries own the physical artifacts, which can be viewed in person by researchers, they do not own the intellectual property, and libraries may be reluctant, due to possible copyright infringement, to make the materials more accessible such as making digital images available on the Internet. As of this writing, for instance, UCLA is sharing only a fraction of the digital version of its Strachwitz Frontera Collection of Mexican and Mexican American Recordings because "it believes most of the collection is made up of orphans." Other institutions have chosen directions with regard to orphan works. After performing due diligence in trying to confirm copyright, the University of California at San Diego chose to make digital images of its Scripps Institution of Oceanography Archives available nationally by "putting orphans under the shelter of fair use."[7] Currently, the scholarly and librarian communities are seeking congressional action to liberalize access to orphan works. Until the copyright status of orphan works is resolved, however, libraries will have to consider each situation on a case-by-case basis.

Copyright compliance is ultimately the responsibility of the library user. Although rare book librarians can alert users about copyright law and, in some cases, refuse to reproduce materials that appear to violate copyright law, they cannot, in the end, control how a library user utilizes research notes. The rare book library can, however, require completion of a research application that should include a statement on copyright provision. Such a statement not only fulfills the library's ethical responsibility to inform its researchers but also abrogates the library from complicity should copyright violation occur.

THE IMPORTANCE OF COPYRIGHT

The purpose of copyright is to protect individual and corporate intellectual properties in order to promote initiative and innovation in the arts and humanities. Because compliance with the U.S. Copyright Law is both a legal and ethical responsibility, rare book librarians need to stay up-to-date on copyright law, especially as it pertains to their collections and the acquisition of new materials.

NOTES

1. Marc Parry's article "Supreme Court Takes Up Scholars' Rights" from *The Chronicle of Education* (June 3, 2011) reports on an upcoming Supreme Court case where a musical conductor at the University of Denver (and other plaintiffs) are challenging a change in copyright law "that moved vast amounts of material from the public domain back behind the firewall of copyright protection." Without going into detail, the plaintiffs contend that the outcome of the case "will touch a broad swath of academe for years to come, dictating what materials scholars can use in books and courses without jumping through legal hoops."

2. For a good historical view of U.S. copyright law, see G. Thomas Tanselle. "Copyright Records and the Bibliographer" in *Selected Studies in Bibliography* (Charlottesville: University Press of Virginia, 1979), 93–140.

3. See http://www.copyright.gov/circs/.

4. WATCH can be accessed online at http://tyler.hrc.utexas.edu/index.cfm.

5. Ironically, the *Ian Hamilton Working Papers for J. D. Salinger: A Writing Life, 1934–1988* are available and accessible at the Princeton University Manuscripts Division, including uncorrected proofs of the unpublished work (http://diglib.princeton.edu/ead/getEad?eadid=C0714&kw=). But, as advised above, though a researcher may view the materials, he or she will be unable to quote from them.

6. Robert A. Gorman, "Copyright and the Professoriate: A Primer and Some Recent Developments," *Academe* 73 (September-October 1987): 32.

7. The examples from the UCLA and University of California at San Diego collections are from Marc Parry, "Out of Fear; Colleges Lock Books and Images away from Scholars," *The Chronicle of Higher Education* (June 3, 2011). http://chronicle.com/article/Out-of-Fear-Institutions-Lock/127701/.

FURTHER READINGS

Code of Best Practices in Fair Use for Academic and Research Libraries. The Association of Research Libraries. January 2012. http://www.arl.org/pp/ppcopyright/codefairuse/code/index.shtml

Hirtle, Peter. "Copyright Term and the Public Domain in the United States." Copyright Information Center, Cornell University. 1 January 2012. http://www.copyright.cornell.edu/resources/publicdomain.cfm.

Jaszi, Peter, et al. "Fair Use Challenges in Academic and Research Libraries." The Association of Research Libraries. 20 December 2010. http://www.arl.org/bm~doc/arl_csm_fairusereport.pdf.

Vaidhyanathan, Siva. *Copyrights and Copywrongs: The Rise of Intellectual Property and How It Threatens Creativity*. New York: New York University Press, 2003.

CHAPTER 10

Outreach

PART I. FINDING AND WORKING WITH YOUR LOCAL COMMUNITIES

THE MYTH OF THE CAPTIVE AUDIENCE

In the nature of things the books housed in rare book collections will tend to be among the less heavily used material possessed by the library—and it is proper (indeed vital, from the conservation angle) that this should be so. Nevertheless, in a time when libraries' costs are rising and their incomes are not . . . the risks for lightly used materials which require special housing and handling are clear. . . . If the value of such collections is not recognized and supported by government and by society at large, the future is unpromising.

—Roderick Cave.[1]

Although written three decades ago, the statement above applies just as much today as it did then. No librarians should take for granted that the value of the collections for which they care is evident to those outside the library's walls. Nor should they believe that their local community is their library's captive audience. This is especially true of rare book libraries and other special collections, the value of which might not be apparent to most.

Take for example, an editorial written in the midst of the recent recession by a student for his university paper suggesting that the library sell some of its rare material to raise needed funds. As librarians, our first impulse is to take offense and become defensive. What an ignorant lout. How dare he not know how primary resources support the research of faculty in a university community? Well maybe he does not know. And whose fault is that? Upon reflection, a more measured response could be to admit that sometimes such opinions stem from a lack of outreach on the part of librarians.

A librarian should not assume that a student knows the value of the library's rare collections. Moreover, a librarian should not assume that the library administration, university or college president, and state senators know the value of the library's collections. If the library staff is not letting its community know what services it provides and the value of such services, then they cannot be upset when members of its community do not see the value in simply housing old and expensive artifacts. From students to the university president, from state senators to the state governor, your community needs to know something about your library. If you have done successful outreach, your reputation should precede you.

Even in cases when a library's reputation is strong, there is always work to be done. For example, there are a surprising number of people who think that the Folger Shakespeare Library in Washington, D.C., is only a collection of Shakespeareana rather than a rich library of books, manuscripts, art, and special collections from early modern Europe. Moreover, user traffic may be high at the Folger, but that does not mean that all the library's resources are visible to users and being used. Outreach still has to be done to draw attention to the lesser-known and underused materials. Rare book librarians at every institution must reach out to their local communities and beyond.

WORKING WITH FACULTY

Most rare book libraries are affiliated with colleges or universities and have a vested interest in close relations with faculty and curriculum. Even those rare book libraries that function independently and autonomously are most often frequented by the academic world. In brief, by the nature of their mission, scholars and researchers are and always will be the principal, mainstay constituency of rare book libraries.

Reach Out to Faculty

Librarians who are subject specialists—English, history, science, language librarians—have a natural constituency to rely upon for advice and guidance and a support group during fiscal or other crises. Rare book librarians, because they represent all areas of knowledge, do not always have a natural constituency among the teaching faculty of the college or university. Rare book librarians should seek out those faculty scholars (including graduate students) who use the collections and look for opportunities to engage their interest in mutually rewarding activities. Also, as part of an ongoing outreach program, rare book librarians should identify those faculty members who are not using the rare book collections and encourage such use. Thus, high on the to-do list of all newly hired rare book librarians should be to contact academic departments in the disciplines that could be served by the library's holdings and arrange to attend departmental meetings in order to introduce themselves and their library's holdings.

Rare book libraries are meant to be used, and outreach to faculty is the first step to demystifying the perception, unfortunately still prevalent, that the rare book room is exclusive, a sanctum sanctorum. This perception may even exist among other library colleagues. Engagement with teaching faculty also offers the opportunity for greater engagement with library colleagues from other departments—subject areas, user education, digital resources, technical services—and promotes involvement with the larger library community. The most obvious strategy is to make the rare book room an integral part of the teaching experience whenever possible. Class sessions scheduled for the rare book room may be the first experience that students will have had with primary materials and original documents. Sessions like this offer rare book librarians the opportunity to not only display the unique collections to a future constituency but also begin to develop in them the understanding of the importance of primary materials for advanced research. As noted, such sessions can involve library colleagues and demonstrate further the compatibility and enrichment that rare books add to the learning experience. Making history tangible is a fundamental way of imparting your library's mission of acquiring, preserving, and making rare books accessible.

Host Open Houses and Co-Teach Courses

Invite faculty to visit your library. Host open houses where a selection of material is presented to scholars and students from a particular academic department or in a particular field. You will be surprised to learn that some faculty on college or university campuses just assume that there is nothing in the rare book collection to support their research. This may be true, but it should never be assumed. Inviting your community into your library results in an increased awareness of your collections. Sometimes professors and students are introduced to potential research projects, and professors may begin to see how their courses might incorporate rare materials.

If you are interested in teaching, you should approach a member of the appropriate faculty to co-teach a course that draws on library holdings. Don't wait for faculty to approach you about any of these possibilities. Be proactive. Stay abreast of the latest course offerings, keeping an eye out for topics that you know your collections support. Professors, who may not have co-taught or incorporated rare materials into their courses, may welcome your assistance, so never be shy about offering your support.

Form an Advisory Committee

Another way to involve faculty with rare books is to form an advisory committee that advises and supports your library. Typically, such a committee would be comprised of faculty from diverse disciplines with particular emphasis on those academic departments whose research and teaching reflect the areas of strength within the rare book collections. As the convener of such a body, the rare book librarian, on a periodical basis, has the opportunity to apprise the constituent faculty on the acquisitions, collection development initiatives, programming, and other activities of the rare book department. Committee members then serve as liaisons between their departments and the rare book library, possibly leading to further contacts among faculty. Conversely, faculty committee members can communicate to the rare book library the activities of their departments such as new hires and their teaching and research interests, new courses, programs, initiatives, and grants: areas of academic development that could be assisted by the rare book library. For faculty members, serving on an advisory committee might be a unique and enjoyable way of helping to fulfill their service obligation to their university or college communities.

Although not all faculty will cultivate relationships, it has been the experience of most rare book librarians that there will always be a number of research and teaching faculty who will be eager to work with the rare book library in a variety of roles, such as grant writing, fund-raising, team teaching, publications, and editorial assistance.

WORKING WITH STUDENTS, OR, YOU'RE NEVER TOO YOUNG TO LOVE RARE BOOKS

Linking up with faculty is the path to working with students, one of the most rewarding aspects of librarianship. Any librarian who has ever had the opportunity of introducing rare books to students can attest to the joy of watching the awe and amazement as they turn the pages of centuries-old artifacts. The first question is typically, "Can I really touch this?" Curious questions follow. "What's the paper made of?" "Can *you* read these letters?" "Who owned this book?" Such questions could very well be the beginning of a life-long love of rare books. Students might be lured into a career in a library, archive, or museum. They might become book collectors; perhaps some might eventually donate their collection to a library. They might become scholars who conduct archival-based research. Or perhaps they might simply continue to support libraries as friends of the library. Such results come from the powerful impact of showing real historical artifacts to young people.

The good news is that libraries are increasingly seeing the potential in outreach to younger students. A *New York Times* article from October 30,

2008, written by Roger Mummert, spotlights the University of Pennsylvania's rare book librarian John Pollack and his work with undergraduates. Appropriately titled, "Handle This Book!," Mummert's article reports that rare books

> are being incorporated into undergraduate courses at institutions like the University of Iowa, Smith College, the University of Washington and Harvard. Last academic year, almost 200 classes and student tours visited the rare-books collection of the University of Pennsylvania. That's almost three times the number of visitors five years ago.[2]

In the article, Pollack expresses an important sentiment expressed by many current rare book librarians, "We're not running a museum." Rare book collections are working collections. They are laboratories for scholars *and* students.

Hire Student Workers

The most personal contact students will have with rare books might come through library jobs and internships. Hiring student workers requires the same vigilance needed for any new hire who will be provided with access to rare and valuable materials. But once you have found the right fit, student workers can be a great asset to rare book libraries and other special collections. You will find that they are capable of high-level work and want to be challenged. They may get grumpy about mundane tasks (who does not?), but once they are trained to perform more professional work, their talents will surprise you. The authors of this book have seen students excel at descriptive bibliography, digital photography, and reference work. All of these tasks build on a student's talents and curiosity. We have even seen students flourish in the field of conservation to the extent that they were building clamshell boxes and treating books needing minor repair. Students from different backgrounds also bring fresh insights and innovative ideas (particularly when it comes to the digital world). So do not shut them out. Do your best to provide them with opportunities to provide real input. Having students present in your reading room also can make the environment more comfortable and welcoming for other students who may wish to use your resources, but find your library somewhat intimidating.

Think of Creative Ways to Involve Students

Getting students interested in rare books can also be done through more creative approaches. Some libraries host book-collecting clubs. For example, The Rare Book & Manuscript Library of the University of Illinois at Urbana-Champaign sponsors The Harris Fletcher Book Collecting Award and T. W. Baldwin Prize for Book Collecting, two annual contests held simply "to foster the love of books."[3] The former award goes to an undergraduate, the latter to a graduate student. The library also established the book-collecting club called The No. 44 Society, which is open to everyone in the university and local communities. A love of books could also be fostered by creating a student organization devoted to rare books. You might hold informational workshops on more popular subjects like printing, papermaking, or artists' books. You could start up a reading club devoted to books about books. There are endless possibilities if you use your imagination.

WORKING WITH LOCAL COMMUNITIES

University libraries should extend their reach beyond the campus to local communities. This kind of outreach is a necessity for librarians working in public and independent research libraries. Create a reputation for holding exciting special events. This could be a series of lectures, concerts, or films. Marathon readings of famous books have become popular. Host a reading of a book that is of special interest to your library or community. For example, a marathon reading of Sarah Orne Jewett's *Country of the Pointed Firs* held at the University of Maine's Fogler Library in the fall of 2000 brought attention to the library's Jewett holdings. Participants included professors, students, friends of the library, and interested locals. At each event be sure to have appropriate items from your collection on display. This could be in the form of a current exhibition or a temporary display supporting the event. Exhibitions are crucial outreach tools and will be discussed in part three of this chapter.

One of the purposes of outreach to your local communities is to familiarize them with your resources. Another is to assure them that they can have access to your collections (if indeed your library is open to the public) and to inform them of how to become users. Your local library patrons might feel nervous about knocking on your door. Make them feel welcome. Many may still have the old perception of rare book libraries as impenetrable fortresses run by stodgy old souls wanting not to be disturbed. Rare book libraries should always be secure spaces, to be sure, but not impenetrable, nor unwelcoming. Getting potential users through the door is sometime a difficult but potentially rewarding first step in a long journey.

WORKING WITH FRIENDS

Donor relations and development are an essential component of every rare book library both proactively and reactively. That is to say, rare book librarians most typically nurture a network of donors and potential donors. At the same time, it is natural for people with rare books to offer collections to rare book libraries. Good donor relations require tact, patience, tolerance, and general bonhomie. There are situations when a rare book curator will befriend and nurture a potential donor for years with no results; there are other situations when gifts, either money or materials, will come with little effort, perhaps even unsolicited. Although unsolicited gifts have come, undoubtedly, to every rare book library at one time or another, reliance upon serendipity is foolhardy, and a reasonable collection development plan should be in place and available for view by possible donors.

Of first and foremost importance is the creation and growth of a reliable donor base and ongoing outreach to potential friends and supporters. And, lest we seem to stress too strongly the financial relations of rare book supporters, we must emphasize that friends of a library can serve it fruitfully in a variety of roles. Certainly, financial support is greatly appreciated and most generally accepted, though we will talk later on about proffered gifts with unreasonable demands. But we cannot expect that all friends of the rare book library are in a material position to benefit the library financially or through great collections. Yet, there are numerous services that can benefit the operations, promotion, and publicity of the library.

Most libraries, even some of the most affluent, are normally not blessed with extensive funds for consistent and timely promotional efforts; friends of the library can bring skill sets—technical, literary and artistic, design, social, and so on—that can augment, refine, and expand fund-raising efforts, public events, or exhibits. The services may be advice and counsel drawing upon the friends' lifetime of experience operating in the public and private sectors. They can provide strategies and define goals as valuable as consulting, at considerable cost, with professional public relations or advertising firms. They can assist in designing catalogs and brochures, posters and circulars, proofreading newsletters, creating and maintaining websites and databases, and manning information booths. And this is not to overlook mundane, though eminently useful, tasks such as setting up chairs or addressing invitations.

An often-underappreciated contribution of supporters is their actual, physical presence at public events. Such events are planned to promote the library and attract more adherents, and it can be counterproductive and embarrassing if the audience is small. Even if the audience is comprised of old friends without a single new face in the house, the circumstance remains an opportunity to develop camaraderie and further enrich organizational relations. If newcomers are attracted to the event with a large and loyal audience, they will sense the importance of the rare books to a vibrant and appreciative community, and, perhaps, choose to become part of it. Consequently, perhaps the most important role for library supporters is the nurturing of other supporters, i.e., establishing an ever-expanding contact base.

In most cases, every rare book library will have adherents who support the library to various extents, from simply using the library (and, yes, patronage is often the first engagement for potential friends) to participating in rare book events and activities to supporting acquisitions, conservation, or operations. In many libraries, there may be a Friends of the Library group already in place, an organization that we will discuss further below. Still, whatever the population of a library support group, it is always good to add to it, both in expanding the base numbers, but also in developing diversity and areas of interest within the support group.

As noted above, it is not expected that this group is developed solely for donations, though donations will likely occur through the halo effect of goodwill and intellectual and emotional engagement, but rather for development of an ongoing source of encouragement and heartfelt exchange. An important component of outreach is not only the necessity of *maintaining* a support group but also expanding it because people move on, become overwhelmed with other interests, such as career and family, and, if the unflattering truth be known, simply tire of the group. And, though old friends retain the sense of tradition and history of an organization, new members bring fresh ideas and innovation: the constant dynamic of keeping the best of the old while incorporating the best of the new.

"Friends of the Library"

In comments above, we have been talking about friends individually, but there is also the "Friends of the Library," as a unified and codified organization, which we will subsequently identify with a capital F. Friends of the Library groups have always existed, either formally or informally, but the Friends movement expanded greatly in the 1960s and, in fact, were part of a general social movement to support the humanities and the arts. Friends groups may generally function for the greater library system at large, but there are cases of Friends groups directed toward specific areas of the library such as rare books. Though sounding somewhat elitist, rare book and special collections departments are stewards of the treasures of most libraries and are therefore natural focuses for development efforts that Friends groups commonly sponsor and support. Even if the mission of the Friends is to support the activities of all areas of the library, again, by the nature of its collections, rare book departments can be prominent participants in Friends' activities. Of course, as with other areas of development and donor relations, the amount of involvement with Friends will be generated, for the most part, by the rare book librarian, for, from experience, Friends groups are almost universally responsive to overtures from those they seek to benefit.

The rare book librarian, however, must be cautious and tactful in the universal acceptance of support proffered by Friends. Undoubtedly, most overtures of support are made with the best of intentions, but Friends groups members, who may be successful and prominent community members, may not clearly understand the mission of the rare book library, the extent of its resources for undertaking major initiatives, the public image that the rare book library strives to perpetuate, or other priorities and development plans. Many, probably most, suggestions from Friends will be sound, manageable, and enriching, and it is the prudent and endearing rare book librarian who will welcome and support positive and productive ideas for fundraising, public relations, and outreach. But, as a closing, iterative caveat, the Friends group must serve as an advisory group, not a policy group, and the rare book library as a department, and in concert with library administration and other affiliated groups (including the Friends, by the way), must clearly articulate its mission and vision, in terms of the collections, services, personnel, and so on, that the Friends can most saliently support.

WORKING WITH DONORS

It is a truism in the development world that though it is better to give than to receive, at the same time, it is also easier to give than to receive. Too often, well-intentioned individuals wish to donate materials that may neither reflect the strengths of the current rare book collections nor promise that the potential donation might develop further. One should be careful, however, in rejecting gifts lest such action jeopardize a richer relationship that might lead to other rewards. Many people like to give, whether for some spiritual or moral satisfaction, gratitude or indebtedness to an institution or an individual, or for tax or other financial purposes. For whatever reason, rejection of a gift, even if the rejection can be explained logically, can create resentments exactly at the juncture when an incipient relationship might be in the making.

In some cases, a donor may not be particular about where a collection ultimately resides, but rather, is concerned about access to and conservation of the collection as an intellectual construct. The donor may first approach a rare book library because it is local or it is his/her alma mater, but the donor is amenable to placing the collection at the most appropriate library. Again, and we will restate this *ad infinitum*, all donor relations must be handled with patience and tact. That is to say, that if a gift in kind is offered that fits neither the current collections nor future mission of the library, nor supports faculty research or other institutional programming, outright rejection should *not* be the first, knee-jerk response. Rather, the donor should be engaged in a discussion of the collection—how did it originate, the extent of it, what are the high spots, what are the plans for its final disposition, and so forth—with intermittent comment about the rare book library. Lest this engagement sound like a ploy, it is akin to the way in which further information is gathered through a reference interview. Oftentimes a donor may not be certain about his or her plans for their collection, and your conversation may help put things into perspective. (There are also situations when you might find it useful to enlist the assistance of a colleague on a donor visit: while you discuss the donation with the donor, your colleague can assess the nature, extent, and condition of the collection at hand.) It benefits rare book librarians, then, to be aware of other library collections in order to suggest possibilities for donation elsewhere; i.e., consider the larger world of research and the value to the scholarly community.

Gifts Are Never Really Free

This is not to suggest that rejection of in-kind donations is a matter of course: far from it. Rather, it is to advise that in-kind gifts are never really free. If we consider processing only, a large collection can require thousands of hours of work at the cost of tens of thousands of dollars. Also, in the expanding world of library materials, physical space is a pressing concern for most libraries especially in light of the cost of storage space.[4] In the end, however, a rare book library's mission is to collect, conserve, and make accessible knowledge and cultural history, and all prospective leads should be explored and acted upon as the situation requires. Although many telephone calls, e-mails, and snail mail communications may be dead ends, what may seem an unpromising lead might be surprisingly productive.

Follow Leads

Every rare book librarian is familiar with the old Bible inquiry. As cherished as a family Bible may be to its owner, a Standard Revised Edition Bible from 1910 is neither rare nor intrinsically valuable unless there are impeccable association values. Such a call regarding old Bibles and other religious works was received at Ohio State. Unlike numerous other calls, however, the courtesy of defining the exact nature of the collection rather than rejecting it outright led to the knowledge that the earliest dated book in the collection was 1521!

Even when there is an apparent fit between a donation and an established collection, few gifts arrive without strings attached. Generally, an institution pledges the ongoing care of the collection. There may well be the further commitment to build upon the collection. Beyond that, there may be additional donor expectations that cannot be reasonably met, although promises can be made to explore funding possibilities. These expectations can be far reaching and include digitization, exhibitions, and fellowships for visiting scholars. A collection of exceptional value may cloud a rare book librarian's judgment and we can only exhort that, as in all areas of donor relations, prudence and caution prevail. This is not to suggest a blasé attitude, for certainly interest and enthusiasm toward a potential gift are nurturing qualities and may form the basis for enduring and expansive donor relations.

Most commonly, gifts-in-kind are stand-alone donations with varying future involvement by the benefactor. Donors may be active, moderate, or inactive participants in the further development of the collection. In light of a donation, it is difficult to solicit extra funding, especially if the gift-in-kind is of outstanding value. Still, although some might perceive it as forward or presumptuous, we do not feel that it is an untoward gesture to open a discussion about a supplemental financial gift to support processing, collection development, and preservation of a collection. In fact, for too long, perhaps, institutions have too readily accepted gifts that will incur ongoing costs and commitments at the sacrifice of other collections and services. Again, illustrations of such situations are innumerable and contingent upon the policies of individual institutions, specific relations of the donor and library, and future plans.

Despite all admonitions regarding wariness at accepting gifts that can come with strings attached and can create compelling obligations and responsibilities that may hamper a library's efficient operations, there can also be occasions when gifts may be just too important to turn away. Every institution has tales of legendary gifts, in some cases world-class collections, that, beyond their intrinsic value alone, may be a fit for other collections' strengths, faculty research, or the library's mission. In addition, these donations may become magnets for other like collections that match favorably with established chronological, geographical, or subject collections and, thus, make each concomitant collection that much stronger. We sometimes think too strongly of highlighted collections, such as a Shakespeare collection, and, though such collections are of extensive worth and distinction, other collections of focused, intellectual design, for instance, can offer new avenues of research and scholarship.

One recent donation to the Rare Books and Manuscripts Library of The Ohio State University Libraries epitomizes the near perfect conjunction of donor intent, research interests, and ongoing commitment coupled with sheer serendipity. Without going into great detail, the serendipity, which was good fortune for Ohio State, was based on the exercising of those various admonitions noted above, i.e., two separate institutions turned the collection away because it did not fit with current policy and institutional commitment. In one case, a new library director did not want to take on a large print collection at a time when the policy for the new library was to devote more financial support for electronic resources. At a second library, astoundingly, a faculty member determined that the collection was not important to the institution's research needs.[5] The eponymous Jerry Tarver Rhetoric, Oratory and Elocution Collection had been developed over the years by the forenamed Dr. Tarver, now emeritus Professor of Speech and Rhetoric at the University of Richmond. The collection numbered over 3,000 titles, with its greatest strength being in nineteenth- and twentieth-century rhetoric. Wishing, in best scholarly fashion, to make this collection available for research, Professor Tarver, after two rejections, contacted a noted scholar of rhetoric at Ohio State. From there it was a quick call to the Rare Books and Manuscripts Library, another call between the library and Professor Tarver, a visit to the University of Richmond, and, ultimately, the placement of the collection at Ohio State.

We cite this particular donation because of how everything went right: relations between the donor and the institutional representatives were highly amicable; a focus of research at the institution (rhetoric and literacy studies) fit with the focus of the collection; and current collections (nineteenth-century children's science, trade catalogs, and advertising) promoted common ideas of the period that expanded the pedagogical features of each individual collection. A subsequently invited lecture by the donor to a local bibliophilic society and meetings and luncheons with involved faculty further cemented relations and led to an established endowment that, in its generosity, was not limited to rhetoric books solely but to rare books generally.

Interacting with Donors

In the optimism of success, it must be pointed out that equal or even greater efforts sometimes lead nowhere, for reasons that may have nothing to do with individuals or institutions but perhaps timing or conflicting interests. Whatever the reason, the variety of experiences does segue to a discussion of development style and to the point that there probably is no single development style that works perfectly in all situations. To some extent, rare book librarians will adopt their style for each individual donor, but in the end, they must to their own selves be true. From quiet dignity to unbridled enthusiasm, from intellectual reserve to ingenuous affection, personalities will vary from individual to individual and each will have endearing attractions for the variety of personalities that exist among the community of donors. This is not to say that a highly emotional curator will not have success with a pleasant, yet detached businessman, for there are more factors than personality in play with donor relations.

As noted, honesty and directness are attributes that build trust and loyalty. Regardless of personality, a donor may simply have a love for the institution, but must be convinced that his intentions will be honored. From the rare book librarian's perspective, the best he or she can do is persuade the donor that a collection or an endowment will be an admirable fit for the institution's mission, such as its programming and research agendas. Moreover, it should be demonstrated that, for in-kind collections, they will be accessible and preserved for perpetuity. If it is a world-class collection, as a category discussed earlier, it can stand on its own as an important research resource; however, with smaller or less-focused collections, they should enhance and enrich collections already in place, i.e., build upon strengths. There can be a tendency for rare book and special collections librarians to be overly acquisitive for the sake of increasing the size of the collection at the expense of research and scholarship. Every library, even the greatest libraries in the world, cannot collect everything, and it is a service to the library profession and national and international librarianship to emphasize collection coherence and strengths and not indulge too widely in exotica or curiosities that detract from the primary responsibilities of the institution.

There are ideals to collection building that must be considered in donor relations, but there are also the realities of tradition, loyalty, and future development. Truthfulness, then, remains the most salient quality of good donor relations. Although donor relations do, indeed, require promotion of an institution, they need not descend into empty promises and vainglorious rhetoric. The *ACRL Code of Ethics for Special Collections Librarians* is clear on the limits of services, including appraisals, that librarians can provide donors, and that document should be reviewed by every rare book librarian on a periodic basis.[6] Yet, beyond the conflicts of interest or breaches of ethics that can occur in donor relations, there may be other donor expectations that exceed the capabilities or even policies of an institution, and the rare book librarian should be wary in compromising the truth for the desire of an acquisition. In the long run, unfulfilled promises will be far more damaging than upfront candidness regarding what an institution or individual can offer the donor.

For instance, inveterate collectors frequently have the vision of their collection existing together physically as a coherent whole for perpetuity. They may envision the collection in specially constructed bookshelves or housed in a dedicated room. In some cases, such a scenario can be satisfied, but normally not without great expense and usually with extra-institutional support from the donors themselves. Certainly there are grand examples of such collections that did receive special accommodations under the funding of the donor, from entire libraries, such as the Folger Shakespeare Library, Pierpont Morgan Library, or Huntington Library, to buildings or rooms within other institutions such as the Scheide Library at Princeton or the Hyde Collection of Samuel Johnson at Harvard. But, in the quotidian world of most rare book librarians, such accommodations are unreasonable. First and foremost, libraries are usually arranged according to a standardized classification system, most commonly the Library of Congress classification or the Dewey Decimal System, that were scientifically created for the logical organization of knowledge: no small task and remarkable for their precision in locating and identifying single books within a collection of even millions. Explained correctly, we would hope that most donors would understand the impracticality of housing dozens, scores, or even hundreds of discrete collections as individual units as opposed to collections being integrated into one general collection. Service delays, for instance, would abound for retrieval, and reshelving alone would severely affect the efficient operations of any large library. Should the donor ever wish to see his or her library reassembled, the technology of the modern electronic catalog can assist in the intellectual arrangement of donated collections through searchable "gift of" notes that can harvest the original donation in its entirety. Such technological capabilities can assuage a donor's disappointment at the physical dispersal of a collection while at the same time enabling access for such things as special exhibitions.

Acknowledging Gifts

Depending on the situation, rare book librarians may wish to express their gratitude to donors in ways that go beyond the traditional written acknowledgment. It may be as simple as placing a bookplate acknowledging the donor into each donated book. Donors sometimes like knowing that their name will continue to be attached to their gifts. A gift note could be added to the online catalog record for donations; the donor can access such records at home and show them to children, grandchildren, and friends. Indeed, if the donation is a large collection, the library might want to name the collection in honor of the donor. For example, The Ohio State University's Stanley J. Kahrl Renaissance and Restoration Drama Collection is named after the generous Ohio State professor who donated his collection of 500 printed books and plays to the university. The donation of large collections such as the Kahrl Collection may call for a special exhibition that serves to announce and promote the use of the donation. Major donations should be publicized in your institution's various publications, the local media, and, if appropriate, the national media. Exhibitions and media attention not only highlight the collection and your library, they may help attract new donors.

Deaccessioning

Deaccessioning is a current issue of extreme importance in all areas of donor relations. Be it important art donated to museums or important collections and materials donated to libraries, donors frequently express concern and exasperation that upon a donation, they cede rights to ownership, and their gifts, so long a part of their lives, may be sold as institutions face fiscal hardships accentuated by economic downturns. On the one hand, donors are absolutely correct in their trepidations because deaccessioning occurs all too frequently. On the other hand, librarians can demonstrate a strong rationale for the practical reasons for deaccessioning under special conditions that are not motivated by economics alone, e.g., limited and marginalized importance of a collection, anomalies, or abandonment of programs.[7]

Related to deaccessioning, it should be remembered that donors, with sincere appreciation for their generosity, do receive rewards for their benevolence through tax benefits. In fact, there is an actual donation strategy called "bargain basement," where an institution can negotiate a combination of cash purchase and donation wherein the government, via tax deductions, essentially contributes to the purchase. (As a side note, though it may seem obvious, we cannot overestimate how important it is that you also advise any donor to consult with his or her own attorney and accountant regarding any donation.) The library ultimately does make a financial commitment by assuming the role of steward of the donated collection, a role that requires real costs including processing, service, and storage. The rare book librarian, then, needs to balance the precarious diplomacy of nurturing sound and enduring relations with donors without ceding control of institutional policies and procedures.

In the end, the institution knows its mission and collection development goals, and the rare book librarian should communicate such policies clearly. Avoiding the temptation of immediate gratification through knee-jerk promises that cannot be kept may well lead to stronger, long-term relations that may yield other benefits over the years. Ideally, if institutional administration will approve, a deaccession policy should be created and put in force. Such a policy will be reassuring to donors particularly in light of the enduring life of the institution as compared to the temporal careers of rare book librarians. Although each institution will have its priorities and will create a policy individually designed for its local mission, we would make some practical suggestions. First, we would encourage that the deaccessioning initiative begin at the curatorial level and ascend through the administrative levels. The curator is closest to the collection, most familiar with both the immediate and long-term goals of collection development, and, very likely the closest individual to the donors to the rare book library. Second, the higher up the administrative chain, the more likely that individuals may act out of concern for immediate fiscal exigencies, including sale of valuable materials, rather than long-term consideration of collections, which will more likely be stronger at the curatorial level. Regardless, the more checks and balances in the deaccessioning policy, the lesser the opportunity for rash decisions that may be regretted decades later. Finally, and though there may be many other provisions to a deaccession policy, lest it be perceived that the proceeds of a successfully deaccessioned item will be used to cover operational costs of an institution, specific provision can be made that all monies be used to develop other collection strengths and for the conservation of current rare book holdings.

WORKING WITH YOUR DEVELOPMENT OFFICE

Many rare book librarians, especially those at large institutions, will have a development office with which to work. As with so many other partnerships forged with rare book libraries—conservation and pre-servation, cataloging, communications—the rare book librarian should enlist the support of the development officer(s). Although the rare book librarian, through knowledge of the collections and expertise in special col-lections, is the principal contact for donor relations, development officers are trained and experienced in the field and their advice and counsel can be inestimable. In brief, the development office is among the rare book library's best friends and that relationship should be nurtured for several reasons. First, a development officer is the primary source for discussing strategies and long-term plans. Second, they can be expressive represen-tatives of the institution at-large and can bring enthusiasm and encourage-ment to donor functions, from lunches and dinners to larger gatherings. In fact, development officers and the development office can offer suggestions, and, in some cases, tangible support for rare book affairs such as tours, lec-tures, and exhibitions. Third, the development office has broad and diverse contacts within the larger institution, community at large, and, if there is a significant alumni base, among a national constituency. In some cases, there may be a well-researched database of historical and potential donors that can include details, such as family, career, and other interests, which provide useful background information prior to meeting with a potential donor.

Not all donors are originally focused on any particular area of an institu-tion; some simply wish to give generally where funds are most needed or will do the greatest good. To that end, the rare book librarian must educate the development officer as to the goals and general vision for the rare book department in addition to collection strengths, highly used collections, cur-rent initiatives and the history of giving, including specific donors. We do not use the term "educate" in any condescending manner, but purely in the sense of providing information about rare book collections with the under-standing that perceptive and assiduous development officers may, in fact, know very much about the collection. What we are emphasizing is ongoing communication with the development office that signals a progressive part-nership. It is the well-informed and astute development officer who can elicit the interests, even passions, of friends of the institution and direct them toward the rare book library should those potential donors' interests and passions match the library's historical strengths and strategic plans. Essen-tially, the development office generally expands the presence and visibility of the rare book library and, specifically, can connect it to a donor base dedi-cated to the furtherance of the institution. It is not an untoward thought that a development officer speaking to an industrialist or corporate lawyer might discover intellectual interests in the history of science or Victorian literature, which, by chance, might be principal collecting areas of the rare book library.

With the goal of an expanded community presence, the rare book librarian, in conjunction with a development officer, if possible, should think in terms of a development team. The development team should not be confused with a Friends group, though it would be logical to presume that the team members would likely draw from that group. Rather, a development team is comprised of business and community leaders who will advocate for the rare book library and expand its constituency. Further, the development team can provide focus and planning for the rare book library at the community and even national level.

THE IMPORTANCE OF OUTREACH

No librarian should assume that their library has a captive audience. Outreach is always needed to raise the visibility of the library, not only to attract a broad and diverse community of users but to build a network of patrons and friends. An established and engaged rare books constituency will become an enduring source of support for the growth and development of the rare books library.

Good donor relations hinge upon the rare book librarian's knowledge of and love for the collections under his or her stewardship. But, a good steward needs to enlist the services of others in order to expand the presence of rare books to broad and various constituencies. The rare book librarian should engender among others an intellectual understanding and a genuine emotional attachment to the collections and a commitment to a progressive, coherent, and engaging vision and strategic plan.

NOTES

1. Roderick Cave, *Rare Book Librarianship* (London: C. Bingley; Hamden, CT: Linnet Books, 1976), 15.
2. Roger Mummert, "Handle This Book!," *New York Times*, October 30, 2008, http://www.nytimes.com/2008/11/02/education/edlife/rarebks.html.
3. See http://www.library.illinois.edu/rbx/CollectingContest.htm.
4. Each institution has a formula for the cost of storage normally based on dollars per square foot. Such estimates will vary from institution to institution and increase from year to year. That is to say, we do not put forward any specific amount in a general text, but advise that such information, at large institutions, is typically available from a facilities operation department.
5. Faculty involvement can be, at given times, profitable and at others, discouraging. Either way, rare book librarians should continue to promote as good faculty relations as possible.
6. See http://www.rbms.info/standards/code_of_ethics.shtml.
7. Although focused on museums rather than libraries, John W. O'Hagan discusses, lucidly and logically, the case for a deaccessioning in "Art Museums: Collections, Deaccessioning and Donations," *Journal of Cultural Economics* 22: 197–207, 1998.

PART II. REACHING BEYOND LOCAL COMMUNITIES

REACHING COMMUNITIES ONLINE

It goes without saying that the majority of your users will have interacted with your library's website. Rare book librarians need to provide an engaging, descriptive overview of their collections on their website, highlighting their collection's strengths and inviting researchers to make use of their resources. Links to the library catalog and research database need to be clearly visible on your home page. Hours of operation and other helpful information need to be easy to find. This is all web design 101 and expected of good libraries. Much of this is primarily the responsibility of your web designer and/or the web librarian. What the rare book librarian must add is content of further value to current and potential users. With current social media applications, the opportunities for online outreach have never been greater in libraries. As we stated earlier in this book: you are serving your users best when you are meeting their needs and meeting them where they are. They are online. And you need to be, too.

Blogs

It doesn't seem like that long ago when many librarians were asking, "What's a blog?" The earliest library blogs tended to be more about the individual librarian who hosted the blog, or about types of librarians, whether tattooed or naked. Community blogs blossomed in the wake of such early sites as Jenny's Cybrary,[1] librarian.net, and Lisnews.org. Libraries using blogs as a method of outreach followed, though at a somewhat slower pace. For rare book libraries and special collections, the adoption of blogs is relatively recent. Even as late as 2008, the RBMS preconference hosted a seminar titled "Blog Boot Camp: An Introduction to Blogging for Special Collections Staff." Nevertheless, there are now a fairly impressive number of blogs devoted to rare book libraries and special collections more generally.

Blogs are an excellent way of sharing timely information with your local communities and beyond, because they are simple to use and allow the host to publish news, announcements, audio, and video as often as he or she would like, while allowing users to subscribe and be notified when the blog is updated. Libraries can use blogs to announce new acquisitions, upcoming events, and new publications and to spotlight items or collections. You might share more personal news such as staff retirements or new hires, or link to news stories pertaining to rare books or subject matter covered by your collection. The goal is to create a community while generating interest in your collection. The key is to keep the blog up-to-date. A rarely updated blog is a sad sight.

A Sampling of Rare Book Library Blogs

Rare Book Collections @ Princeton (Princeton University Library)
http://blogs.princeton.edu/rarebooks/
Confessions of a Curator (Northern Illinois University)
http://niurarebooks.blogspot.com/
Lilly Library News & Notes (Indiana University Bloomington)
http://www.indiana.edu/~liblilly/blog/
LSU Libraries Special Collections (Louisiana State University)
http://hill.blogs.lib.lsu.edu/
Charles Babbage Institute News and Information (University of Minnesota)
Http://blog.lib.umn.edu/cbi/
The Blogging Libraries Wiki links to as many library blogs as it can find:
Http://www.blogwithoutalibrary.net/links/index.php

Facebook

Blogs are helpful outreach tools, but unless your users are subscribed to your blog and getting updates sent to them, then they have to visit your blog to receive your information. Other avenues offer a more direct relationship with your users. Facebook is currently the most popular social networking website. Used properly it can be an active communications tool. Like a blog, Facebook allows you to post static information such as your mission statement, hours, and contact information, while also posting announcements, images, and video. Once a user friends you, your content will stream directly into their news feed (unless you manage to get hidden or blocked). For many people, checking their Facebook page has become a regular (sometimes obsessive) activity. Getting your content onto your users' news feed is a prime example of meeting your users where they are. But be sure to stay active. Like blogs, Facebook pages need to be dynamic to maintain user interest.

Twitter

Twitter is another social networking application that libraries are increasingly adopting. In some ways, Twitter as a microblogging service is taking over the role RSS feeds have played on blogs in the past, sending information directly to users who have subscribed to receive content. The limited number of characters allowed for each message results in nuggets of information such as: "Hoyt Family Papers available: http://findingaids.cul.columbia.edu /ead/nnc-rb/ldpd_4078915,' " posted at 10:57 a.m. on November 16 on Twitter for Columbia University's Rare Books and Manuscripts Library:

http://twitter.com/columbiarbml. Thus you can send distilled messages, often with a link with further information.

Twitter can be an easy, unobtrusive way of reminding users of your events and services. As with Facebook the challenge is getting your users to sign up. Be sure to promote your presence on these platforms. Mention it during class meetings and other events and have "Like Us On Facebook" and "Follow Us On Twitter" icons on your website and promotional material.

Creating a Second Life for Your Collections

Meeting your users where they are may mean putting your library's digital content in rather unexpected places. In 2009, Stanford University's Special Collections and University Archives moved into the world of virtual reality, creating a Virtual Archives in the popular 3-D virtual world of Second Life.[2] Here, portions of Stanford's collection are presented in digitized facsimiles. Some are hung on walls in a virtual exhibition space. Some are housed in virtual gray Hollinger boxes that the user needs to open up. They have even provided a virtual reference board where users can submit reference questions. Take a quick trip around Stanford's Library Island and you will recognize that there is something to the idea of displaying digitized artifacts in a virtual environment. Potential uses include creating a digital extension of current exhibitions or setting up a virtual environment in which users are allowed to browse stacks that are typically restricted. There is also potential in using virtual reality to serve users at a distance and to even better serve our users who have special needs. There is certainly a future in 3-D facsimiles of materials that provide a more accurate representation of the physical makeup of artifacts. Bold steps like Stanford's Virtual Archives are among the first steps to this future.

SOCIAL METADATA

Social metadata is information about your information that has been contributed by members of your local community and beyond. Perhaps the most famous example of a library inviting social metadata occurred in January 2008, when the Library of Congress joined forces with Flickr and launched The Commons, a Flickr space where museums and archives could place photographs with no known copyright restrictions online to be tagged and commented on by the public. The idea is to provide access to these photos, but also to generate information about them. The Library of Congress originally posted 3,100 photos, and the response was immediate and overwhelming. They received 11,000 tags on their first day.[3]

The thought of someone other than a trained cataloger describing special collections items may still rub some librarians the wrong way. However, special collections and social metadata make a very good match. Our focused collections cater to focused researchers, who typically know more about our artifacts than we do. Why not invite their input? You could invite such contributions by uploading items from your collections onto public sites like Flickr. Closer to home, Next Generation (Next Gen) online public access catalogs (OPACs) are increasingly incorporating applications that enable collection of social metadata, whether in the form of user tags, annotations, or ratings. Imagine an online catalog record for a rare book that includes space for users to share what they know about a book or specifics about that particular copy of the book. They might bring attention to a manuscript note that reads, "This was y^e [*the*] only booke I carried in my pockett when I travelld beyond y^e [*the*] seas y^e [*the*] 22^d year of my Age; & many years after Just. Isha[m]."[4] They might leave a note for other researchers reading, "This book appears to have an interesting provenance and should be studied further." They might use the space to correct any cataloging errors. They might simply tag the record with the term "manuscript annotations."

A site like Washington State University's Plateau Peoples' Web Portal (http://plateauportal.wsulibs.wsu.edu/) demonstrates the types of information a library, archive, or museum can solicit from its users. Documents uploaded to the site include photographs, manuscripts, and printed texts. These documents can be annotated, commented on, tagged, and in the case of the textual material, transcribed. There is also a function for uploading audio and video comments. The site even allows for geotagging, so the location of certain photographs or events can be pinpointed on Google Maps.

The cultivation of social metadata for use in libraries, archives, and museums is a trend that will certainly increase in the coming years, and the applications for capturing social metadata will continue to evolve. OPAC providers will continue to build and refine their Next Gen catalogs and their social applications. The rare book librarian needs to stay on top of these developments and choose the best ways to solicit and use social metadata. Done successfully, you not only acquire descriptive information regarding your collections, you further build your own community. After all, why should your catalog records not be the site for scholarly input and conversation?

REACHING RESEARCHERS

Research Fellowships

"Do you offer fellowships?" Many rare book librarians will have been asked this question many times. The truth is that outreach is sometimes not enough to get scholars through the door. Researchers need resources to travel to specific libraries. Sometimes they can get funding through their home institutions, but usually they are looking for outside funding. Many of the more active research libraries offer fellowships. It is a part of the culture of independent research libraries, which do not having formal local communities to serve as colleges and universities do. Thus, libraries like The Huntington Library, the Folger Shakespeare Library, and the Newberry Library offer dozens of fellowships both long-term and short-term. If your library has strong collections that should be attracting scholars beyond your local communities, then you need to think strongly about offering fellowships. For a modest investment, you may get a substantial return.

Offering even just one fellowship provides the opportunity for outreach that is akin to advertising. Your announcement should be posted on all applicable web boards and lists, whether general in scope or specific to nature of your collections. Printed flyers or e-mail notices should be sent to relevant institutions and academic departments. Such announcements provide the opportunity to describe your collections and perhaps highlight new acquisitions. For example, you may have learned about the Nantucket Historical Association's 2010 E. Geoffrey and Elizabeth Thayer Verney Fellowship through a posting on the ExLibris List.[5] In addition to spelling out the details of this fellowship, the post described the museum's collections. Through this post many ExLibris subscribers learned something substantial about the Nantucket Historical Association and its holdings. By using a listserv in this manner, you can reach quite a large audience, and all for free.

Fellowships are hardly draining on library budgets. Depending on where your library is located, a monthlong fellowship could range between $1,500 and $2,500 to cover travel, lodging, and other expenses. When you think of the outreach that is already done when announcing the fellowship, then the money is already well spent before the researcher even arrives.

The bottom line is the best way to bring attention to your collections is to have them used. It's a bit of a catch-22, but *use spurs more use*. Offering fellowships will plant the seeds. The benefits for outreach do not stop once the research fellows are in residence. If the fellow is satisfied with your holdings and service, he or she will spread the word to others in the scholarly community, particularly those working in the same field. Moreover, when your research fellows publish scholarship based on primary materials in your collections, other scholars in the field will take notice. Use spurs more use.

Announcing New Acquisitions and Highlighting Existing Collections

New acquisitions can also help bring new users to your library. Just as fellowship announcements can serve as free advertising, so, too, can announcements publicizing new acquisitions. Selected listservs are once again useful in this regard. More generally, a press release can be sent to the media outlets typically used by your college or university. You may suggest that the college newspaper and other campus publications write an article about your new acquisitions. Perhaps you just acquired a major collection that will be of great significance to scholars in a specific field. You should attend conferences in that field and present a paper on research opportunities at your library.

Similarly, if your library has strong existing collections that are being underused or overlooked, then you should reach out to the appropriate scholarly community and present them with research opportunities. You may also want to write an article on your collections for an appropriate journal in the field. For example, several articles describing strong sub-collections held at the Folger Shakespeare Library have appeared in selected journals over the decades. Most recently library staff penned a brief article focusing on the library's Slavic and Eastern European holdings.[6]

The acquisitions chapter of this book highlights the idea of building on your collection's strengths. A researcher will not likely visit your library if you only have a few items that he or she needs to consult. Two exceptions are if your library is nearby or has an item that is essential to their research. Otherwise researchers will travel to where there is a critical mass of resources (and where they can apply for fellowships for access to this critical mass). That way they know that their time in residence will be productive. Building on your strengths combined with the right amount of outreach should result in your library gaining recognition as a center for research in your specific fields of strength.

For example, throughout the 1990s, the Rare Books and Manuscripts Library at The Ohio State University built on their strong holdings of printed books documenting the Protestant Reformation. They expanded to collecting editions of John Foxe's *Acts and Monuments* or *Book of Martyrs*, at a time when Foxe studies was becoming a hot historical topic. Outreach followed in the form of an exhibition on Foxe's *Book of Martyrs* in 1999, an NEH seminar on Foxe in 2001, the digitization of Foxe's early work *Rerum in Ecclesia gestarum* (1559) and the first edition of the *Book of Martyrs* (1563), and the contribution of over 200 images from several editions of the *Book of Martyrs* to the American Theological Library Association's Cooperative Digital Resources Initiatives (CDRI) database. All of this work paid off. These days Ohio State is known for being a site for English Reformation and Foxe studies.

THE IMPORTANCE OF ONLINE OUTREACH AND RESEARCH FELLOWSHIPS

Online outreach is about community building. Work to create an online community around your collections and programming. Meeting users where they are includes interacting with them through Facebook and Twitter, and sending updates to your blog through RSS feeds. In addition to providing information concerning your collection, also create platforms through which users can contribute information concerning your collection. After all, your users will know things about your collection that you and your staff do not.

Reaching out to potential users should also mean providing them with opportunities to come to you. In order for scholars to find the time and money to facilitate research in collections held outside their home institutions, they often seek research fellowships. Although they will have opportunities to apply for funding within their own institutions and through major grant and fellowship funding organizations, they will also seek out libraries and archives that offer fellowships. Even the most modest financial commitment towards research fellowships will go a long way toward getting scholars through your door and promoting the holdings of your collection.

NOTES

1. See http://jennyscybrary.lishost.org/.

2. See http://www-sul.stanford.edu/depts/spc/pubserv/outreach2.htm. A video demo may be found at http://www.youtube.com/watch?v=3_TWmth3MdE.

3. Noam Cohen, "Historical Photos in Web Archives Gain Vivid New Lives," *New York Times*, 18 January 2009. http://www.nytimes.com/2009/01/19/technology/internet/19link.html?_r=2&partner=permalink&exprod=permalink.

4. To see this inscription, visit: http://manifoldgreatness.wordpress.com/tag/sir-justinian-isham/.

5. Everett Wilkie, "Fellowship Announcement," 1 December 2009, online posting, ExLibris listserv.

6. Melissa Cook and Steven K. Galbraith, "Hidden Slavic and Eastern European Materials at the Folger Shakespeare Library," *Slavic & East European Information Resources* 2 (2010): 59–63.

PART III. EXHIBITIONS AND EXHIBITION LOANS

Exhibitions are an essential part of outreach for rare book libraries, whether you are mounting an exhibition at your home institution or participating in an outside exhibition by loaning items from your collection. Not only are exhibitions an effective and engaging way of bringing attention to your holdings, they challenge librarians to think creatively about their collections and how to present them to the public. For these reasons, creating exhibitions is one of the most enjoyable aspects of rare book librarianship. Many who go into the field are already imaginative and creative. Choosing exhibition items, designing case layouts, writing case labels, and writing promotional copy can truly bring out the best talents of librarians.

Some rare book libraries are fortunate enough to have their own permanent exhibition space. Some share exhibition space with other library units, campus departments, and community organizations. If your library shares space, be sure that there is a formal exhibition schedule that is planned a few years out and that your library is on that schedule regularly. Opportunities for exhibitions may be limited and thus highly desired, so it is better to be prepared. Even if you have your own exhibition space, it is good to schedule topics two or three years in advance. No matter how small, successful exhibitions take a great deal of planning and organization. Exhibition planning needs to be regular part of your workflow, and needs be reflected in your budget and job descriptions.

CHOOSING EXHIBITION TOPICS

One of the simplest ways to choose exhibition topics is to look at the strengths of your holdings. The Ohio State University's Rare Book and Manuscripts Library holds one of the finest collections of material related to the author William S. Burroughs. Thus, in 2001 the library held an exhibition titled "An American Avant Garde: First Wave" that focused on Burroughs. Among the artifacts chosen for the exhibition were Burroughs's own notebooks and diaries, photographs, and literary manuscripts and typescripts. Burroughs himself seemed to be in the room, as curators filled a vertical glass case with a suit of his clothes, accessorized with his hat, shoulder holster, knife, and paint-splattered shoes. Also featured were Burroughs's own copies of literary works written by other American avant-garde writers. This allowed the exhibition curators to highlight Ohio State's excellent Burroughs collection, while also bringing to attention Ohio State's larger collection of American avant-garde writers.

Exhibitions can also spotlight the recent acquisition of a major artifact or collection. Anytime a library acquires a major purchase or donation, they should follow up the acquisition with outreach to those who are likely to make use of the materials. Announcing new acquisitions on your website and blog and sending announcements to the appropriate discussion lists and message boards are effective ways of bringing attention to new items. When you hold an exhibition you do all of these things, while also displaying and describing the materials to a great many people. One downside that you need to consider is that if the items are in exhibition cases, they are not available for users. This might have some bearing on which items you choose to put in the case. Perhaps you will want to only display a portion of a newly acquired collection and make the rest available for users. Overall, however, you should be focusing more on the future of the collection and the research that will be conducted after the exhibition comes down.

Taking a different tack, ideas for exhibitions can also come from obscure or underused resources in your collection. Every librarian can attest to the fact that there are portions of their collection that they wish would receive more attention. For whatever reasons there are always hidden strengths in libraries. One way to spotlight them is to build an exhibition around them. That might mean a topic-driven exhibition or simply a "from the vaults" exhibition where the overarching theme is simply, "I bet you didn't know our library had these resources."

Finally, one last suggestion for exhibition ideas is to track major upcoming events and anniversaries for potential occasions for exhibitions. If your campus is slated to host the World University Games (Universiade) in a few years, than perhaps you might plan an exhibition on the history of sport. If your town is holding an Irish Festival, then offer to host an exhibition of your Irish materials. Similarly keep an eye out for major anniversaries. In 2005, for example, libraries around the world hosted exhibitions and other events celebrating the 400th anniversary of the publication of Miguel Cervantes's *The Ingenious Gentleman Don Quixote de la Mancha*, one of the most important and influential books ever to be published.

WORKING WITH GUEST CURATORS

Exhibition topics may also reflect the scholarship that is being done on your campus or in your community. Say, for example, there is an active Mark Twain scholar in your community. You may want to invite that person to curate an exhibition on Twain that builds on their current research. Your own collection may provide some of the exhibition materials; the rest can be filled in with exhibition loans (should your budget allow it).

In this way, you can cultivate relationships with local or visiting scholars by inviting them to curate or co-curate an exhibition. Not only is it helpful to have an expert to guide the exhibition (and share the workload), it creates goodwill between your library and the scholar's department or institution. Scholars enjoy curating exhibitions both for the satisfaction of mounting a successful production and for the attention it brings to their research. As you successfully collaborate on exhibitions, you should expect to be approached by other scholars about future potential exhibitions. Be proactive and stay abreast of the research that is being done using your library's materials. Keep an eye out for engaging topics on campus or in your community and beyond.

If your library has a collection that would serve as the foundation of a winning exhibition, but it is a collection not currently being used by researchers, scout out prospective local scholars whose fields of research might be well suited for this collection and approach them about the prospect of curating an exhibition. If no one in your local community fits the bill, consider inviting an outside scholar. You do not need to be looking for an exact fit. Although scholars often actively choose the direction of their research, the right opportunity may send them in new and exciting directions.

Choosing an outside curator involves more than just becoming familiar with a scholar's academic output. You must be sure to choose someone with the right personality for working on an exhibition. You and your staff will be collaborating with this person for a significant amount of time, so choose carefully. Scholars who have never worked on an exhibition often underestimate how much work is involved with putting one on. Although professors are sometimes able to receive research leave to devote to the exhibition, most of the time they will be working on the exhibition on top of their normal workload of teaching, advising, and research. Thus, you need to find someone who will be fully committed to the exhibition and who understands what is expected of them. From the very first meeting, have a sample work schedule and show them exactly what their responsibilities will be. Finding someone with the requisite energy and commitment may be difficult, but it will be worth the wait and the exhibition will be all the better for it.

EXHIBITION PUBLICATIONS

Librarians, curators, and scholars often view the opportunity to curate an exhibition as a chance to add to their curriculum vitae. This is expected and understandable. Tenure and academic promotion can be quite rigorous. For professors, curating an exhibition may not carry as much weight towards promotion as placing an article in a major publication, and it certainly will not compare to publishing a monograph. Therefore, they might find the prospect more appealing if their exhibition produces a publication.

Properly planned and executed, exhibition catalogs can greatly enhance your exhibition. Not only do they expand the content of the exhibition and provide more interpretive support, they give the exhibition life outside the exhibition space and beyond the weeks and months that the exhibition is up. The core of most exhibition catalogs is a pictorial representation of the items used in the exhibition, enhanced with greater textual context than what is permitted on exhibition labels. Catalogs also often include scholarly essays written by exhibition curators and scholars in the field. In one way, you might view exhibition catalogs as a print version of the exhibition that visitors who enjoyed the exhibition can purchase and bring home with them. If your exhibition broke new scholarly ground on a subject or discovered important artifacts, then the catalog might be designed to be a scholarly work unto itself that would be comfortable both in the hands of an exhibition visitor or on the shelf of an academic library.

Exhibition publications range from highly illustrated colorful coffee table books, to straightforward, sparsely illustrated, text-driven works. Much will depend upon the content of your exhibition and its audience. Popular topics may bring in a great number of visitors who want to take a piece of the exhibition home. Some topics are simply more visual than others and may call for a more lavish catalog. The cost of print catalogs can be quite expensive depending on the design, length, and number of illustrations. Because they can be expensive, you probably will not have a catalog published for every exhibition you stage. If your budget does not support these sorts of prices or you cannot find external funding, then you might take a do-it-yourself-approach and produce your own catalog in-house. With the right support staff and the right publishing software, this might be a practical and rewarding solution. Plus do-it-yourself book publishing sites such as Lulu.com and Blurb.com (to name but two) offer exciting possibilities.

Similarly, you might choose to publish a version of your exhibition on your website. This could be in lieu of a catalog or simply as a support for the exhibition. Like an exhibition catalog, a web version of your exhibition will reach a wider audience and give life to your work beyond the exhibition dates. You may also see virtual exhibitions as a part of your online presence, an extension of your digital library. If you can produce the website in-house, it may not even be an expensive endeavor. Depending on your resources, you might consider producing an exhibition website using open-source software designed for online exhibitions like Omeka developed by George Mason University's Center for History and New Media (http://omeka.org/).

The Leab Awards

If you do publish an exhibition catalog and feel proud of your work, you should submit it for the Katharine Kyes Leab & Daniel J. Leab *American Book Prices Current* Exhibition Awards. The Leab Awards "are given for excellence in the publication of catalogs and brochures that accompany exhibitions of library and archival materials, as well as for electronic exhibitions of such materials." See http://www.rbms.info/committees/exhibition_awards/index.shtml.

Each year, the Exhibition Awards Committee of RBMS selects winners from several different categories, reflecting the cost of production. The Leab Awards also have given awards in the categories of printed brochures and electronic exhibitions. Winning a Leab Award will bring greater attention to your exhibition. Even submitting your work gets you listed in on their web page. In addition to the Leab Awards, seek out other awards for catalogs and for design more generally. If you are working with a graphic design company, they will surely have suggestions for you, being already active in submitting their work for awards.

EXHIBITION LOANS

The opportunity to have items from your collections on display in exhibitions outside your walls is always appealing. Such outreach can be invaluable as new audiences will become aware of your holdings. Sometimes this can have unexpected results.

In 2006, the Folger Shakespeare Library contributed a painted portrait to an exhibition called "Searching for Shakespeare" at England's National

Portrait Gallery. The portrait, known as the Janssen portrait, due to early speculation that is was painted by the Flemish artist Cornelis Janssen, is thought by some to be of Shakespeare; thought by others to be of Sir Thomas Overbury. A man named Alec Cobbe attended the exhibition, saw the Janssen portrait, and realized that it closely resembled a portrait painted in 1610 that had lingered in his family's collection for centuries. Three years later, Cobbe and Shakespearean scholar Stanley Wells announced to the world that Cobbe's portrait is the only surviving likeness of the William Shakespeare produced during his lifetime. They further argued that the portrait likely served as the model for the iconic engraved portrait of Shakespeare by Martin Droeshout found in the first folio publication of Shakespeare's works (1623). Needless to say, this discovery shook the Shakespeare world, and a great deal of scholarly controversy followed. One wonders if the Folger had not leant the Janssen portrait to the National Portrait Gallery whether the Cobbe portrait would still be languishing in obscurity.

While the great majority of Shakespeare scholars doubt that the Cobbe portrait is really of Shakespeare, the example demonstrates the value of loaning artifacts. When items leave the safety of your own walls, their travels might produce some interesting results. But safety is the key word here. Despite the immediate attractiveness that each opportunity for an exhibition loan brings, several factors need to be considered when deciding if an item should indeed be loaned.

Should an Item Be Loaned?

Loaning your material to another institution usually presents a good opportunity for outreach, but tread carefully nevertheless. First take a good look at the requesting institution and the nature of their exhibition. Is the institution reputable? What is the topic of their exhibition and do you sense that the end result will be strong? What is the size of the audience they expect will visit the exhibition? Will there be an exhibition catalog and will your item be featured?

Next, you need to be sure that the institution has the resources to take proper care of your item while it is in their custody. What sort of exhibition space do they have? Who will be responsible for cradling or mounting your item in the exhibition case? You must request a facilities report from the institution so that you know exactly under what conditions your item will be kept displayed. Institutions that regularly host exhibitions should have a facilities report already prepared. If not point them to a template provided by the American Association of Museums at: http://iweb.aam-us.org/Purchase/ProductDetail.aspx?Product_code=E802. An older version is available here: *sceti.library.upenn.edu/dreyfus/docs/Standard_Facility_Report.pdf*

Note that your institution should also have completed its own facilities report to be used when requesting loans.

Now take a good look at the item or items requested. What condition are they in? If they are in need of conservation, they probably should not travel or should be treated before traveling. Has the item been on exhibition recently? Although the stress sustained by a book while on exhibition should be minimal, a safe approach is to allow the book that has been on exhibition to rest for three years before putting it on exhibition again. You might find that loan requests for standout items in your collection will come fairly frequently, on top of the need to display these items in your own exhibitions. This means you must be all the more discriminating when deciding if and when it should be loaned.

The requesting institution should pay all the costs associated with the loan, including all shipping fees, and insurance on the item both while in their care and during travel. Some institutions also charge a loan fee to cover the work that goes into preparing an item to be loaned. This includes writing a conservation report before it leaves (and again when it returns) and preparing the item to be shipped or hand-delivered. If your library lacks experience with exhibition borrowing and lending, you may consult *Guidelines for Borrowing and Lending Special Collections Materials for Exhibition (2005)* produced by the Rare Books and Manuscript Section (RBMS) of the Association of College and Research Libraries (ACRL) at http://www.ala.org/ala/mgrps/divs/acrl/standards/borrowguide.cfm. It is important for your library to write up its own guidelines and procedures. There are many online examples for you to consult, including Columbia University, at http://www.columbia.edu/cu/lweb/services/policies/loans_for_exhibits.html, and Harvard University, at http://hcl.harvard.edu/libraries/houghton/exhibition_loan_guidelines.cfm.

SAFELY MOUNTING EXHIBITIONS

Preparing books and other items for exhibitions must be done carefully and to archival standards. Similarly, the cases in which items are housed need to provide stable, safe, environments during the entirety of the exhibition. If your library has an in-house conservation staff, they should be participating in mounting your exhibitions. If you lack these resources, then you must learn how to display books and flat items safely. The techniques do not require advanced conservation training and can be handled successfully by librarians and curators. One helpful resource to consult is the chapter on "Small Exhibitions" in Nelly Balloffet and Jenny Hille's *Preservation and Conservation for Libraries and Archives* (Chicago: American Library Association, 2005).

MARKETING AND PROGRAMMING

The effort put into an exhibition demands significant efforts in marketing. You do not want your work to pass with little notice. Be sure that your exhibition is included in all your community's local papers, tourist publications (print and web), and community websites and bulletins. Reach out to groups that might have a particular interest in your exhibition. If your topic is modernist writers, seek out the community of scholars working in that field. Audiences are more diffuse than ever, so you must actively seek them. Go to where they are. Post on their Facebook pages and message boards. Present papers or poster sessions at their conferences. Send invitations directly to institutions and academic departments whose staff would be interested in your exhibition.

Finally, exhibitions provide ample opportunities for programming. If your topic suits particular speakers, authors, or musical groups, then public lectures and performances may augment exhibition content, while increasing exhibition attendance. For example, an exhibition on King Henry VIII held at the Folger Shakespeare Library in 2010 was supported by lectures from scholars, readings from authors of historical fiction, and performances of music associated with Henry's court. The exhibition also provided the opportunity to stage a production of Shakespeare's *Henry VIII*, a play that playgoers rarely have the opportunity to see. Events such as these take time to organize, so again be sure to plan your exhibitions well in advance.

THE IMPORTANCE OF EXHIBITIONS

Exhibitions and exhibition programming may take a great deal of time and energy, but remember that they are excellent and effective opportunities to introduce your community to your collections. They are also opportunities to reach audiences that normally might not come to your library. Library users need not be simply scholars and researchers. They may also be members of the public or tourists that are looking for entertainment and cultural events. Rise to the occasion and create a buzz about your library that extends beyond your walls.

FURTHER READINGS

Barber, Peggy, and Linda Wallace. *Building a Buzz: Libraries and Word-of-Mouth Marketing.* Chicago: American Library Association, 2010.

Crosby, Connie. *Effective Blogging for Libraries.* New York: Neal-Schuman Publishers, 2010.

Dowd, Nancy, Mary Evangeliste, and Jonathan Silberman. *Bite-Sized Marketing: Realistic Solutions for the Overworked Librarian.* Chicago: American Library Association, 2010.

Traister, Daniel. "Public Services and Outreach in Rare Book, Manuscript, and Special Collections Libraries." *Library Trends* 52, no. 1 (2003): 87–108.

Whittaker, Beth M., and Lynne M Thomas. *Special Collections 2.0: New Technologies for Rare Books, Manuscripts, and Archival Collections.* Santa Barbara, CA: Libraries Unlimited, 2009.

Winston, Mark D., and Lisa Dunkley. "Leadership Competencies for Academic Librarians: The Importance of Development and Fund Raising." *College and Research Libraries* 63, no. 2 (2002): 171–182.

CHAPTER 11

Continuing Education

Continuing education is an important part of most occupations and essential for librarians. As practices and standards evolve, so too must your skills and knowledge. Indeed, some of what you learned in library school may no longer be relevant or at the very least needs to be updated. As the previous chapters have shown, rare book librarianship is a dynamic and modern field that is constantly evolving. Best practices in conservation, digitization, and outreach, for example, have changed dramatically in the span of the last decade alone. Rare book librarians also often have the added challenge of contributing to their field as a scholar. A great deal of the continuing education you need you will get on the job, but that is often not enough. A formal commitment to continuing education needs to be a part of the rare book librarian's career path.

THE LIBRARIAN-SCHOLAR

The education qualifications for rare book librarians will vary from job to job. A Master of Library Science (MLS, MLIS) is standard, but some libraries will consider applicants with a PhD in the appropriate subject area. In addition to an MLS, rare book librarians and curators are increasingly expected to have a second master's degree in a suitable field. Moreover, for some jobs the combination of an MLS and PhD is desired. A tall order perhaps, but the field of rare book librarianship is one that values continuing education, whether gained through additional academic degrees or certificates, skills courses, participation in professional organizations, or through research and scholarship.

A commitment to continuing education and professional development is one of the most important qualities of a rare book librarian. Generally speaking, you will find that many people who are attracted to the library field are intellectually curious and keen to gain and share knowledge. This is certainly true of librarians who are working in special collections and archives. They are the kind who take immense joy in caring for objects from the past and present and in working to get a sense of what they mean and how best to provide access to them. In fact, they feel compelled to provide access to the artifacts for which they have been caring. They recognize the importance of their roles as stewards of history. They take pride in being a part of the cultural heritage field.

The term that best describes an active and skilled rare book librarian is "librarian-scholar." This is a librarian who has become a well-trained specialist in his or her subject areas and actively participates in the greater scholarly community by delivering conference papers, participating in professional organizations, and publishing scholarly work. They keep up with current scholarship and interact with the scholars they serve as colleagues in the field, who often seek their input and advice.

In order to function effectively as a librarian-scholar, rare book librarians must be keen to increase their knowledge and skills. With this in mind, assembled below is a list of resources available to librarians who wish to continue their education, whether through formal classes, conferences, or scholarship.

CONTINUING EDUCATION RESOURCES

ALA-Accredited Library Schools

A limited number of library schools maintain a concentration in rare book librarianship. Others may offer a rare books course or cover the topic under a more general special collections course. If you are serious about the field of rare book librarianship, one of the programs listed below might be a good fit for you. Remember that no matter where you study, your classroom training needs to be supplemented with successful internships and practicums. If your library school does not offer a variety of courses in the study of rare books, you might still gain working knowledge through field experience. When choosing a library school, you should look at the libraries, archives, and museums nearby that might offer opportunities in the rare book field.

- School of Library and Information Science, Indiana University
  Bloomington, IN
  http://www.slis.iu.edu/
  Offers a Rare Books and Manuscripts Librarianship Specialization.
  Indiana University is home to the Lilly Library, one of the
  strongest rare book and manuscript libraries in the United
  States.

- Palmer School of Library and Information Science, Long Island University, Brookville, NY
  http://www.liu.edu/palmer
  Offers a Rare Books and Special Collections specialization through their Manhattan location housed at New York University's Bobst Library.
- Graduate School of Library and Information Science, University of Illinois, Champaign, IL
  http://www.lis.illinois.edu/
  http://www.lis.illinois.edu/academics/programs/mbms
  Offers a Certificate in Special Collections through the Midwest Book and Manuscript Studies (MBMS) program.
- School of Library and Information Studies, University of Wisconsin-Madison
  http://www.slis.wisc.edu/
  http://slisweb.lis.wisc.edu/~printcul/
  Courses support a specialization in Book Studies and Print Culture. Madison is home to the Center for the History of Print Culture in Modern America.

Rare Book Schools

Supplementing college and university programs are programs offering intensive courses in subjects related to rare books. Taking courses at these schools is not only an effective way of continuing your education, it provides an excellent route to meeting peers and leaders in the rare books community.

- The Rare Book School, University of Virginia, Charlottesville, VA
  http://www.rarebookschool.org/
  Offers five-day courses throughout the year on a variety of topics related to rare books. Scholarships are available to cover the cost of tuition.
- California Rare Book School, University of California, Los Angeles, CA
  http://www.calrbs.org/
  Offers five-day courses in the summer and fall.
- The London Rare Books School, University of London, England
  http://www.ies.sas.ac.uk/study-training/research-training-courses/london-rare-books-school
  Offers five-day summer courses on book-related topics.
- The Midwest Book and Manuscript Studies (MBMS) program.
  http://www.lis.illinois.edu/academics/programs/mbms
  Offers one- and two-week summer courses.

Societies and Organizations

Participation in professional societies and organizations is a part of professional development. It helps keep you in contact with your peers and up-to-date with current news and activities in the profession. Here are several rare book–related groups that you might want to join:

- American Antiquarian Society, Worcester, Massachusetts: http://www.americanantiquarian.org/
- American Printing History Association: http://www.printinghistory.org/
- The Bibliographical Society of America: http://www.bibsocamer.org/
- The Canadian Association for the Study of Book Culture / Association canadienne pour l'étude de l'histoire du livre: http://casbc-acehl.dal.ca/
- Library History Roundtable (LHRT) of the American Library Association: http://www.ala.org/ala/mgrps/rts/lhrt/index.cfm
- RBMS: Rare Books and Manuscripts Section of the Association of College and Research Libraries (ACRL), a division of the American Library Association (ALA): http://www.rbms.info/
- SHARP: Society for the History of Authorship, Reading and Publishing: http://www.sharpweb.org/

Selected Journals

Keeping up with current scholarship is essential to being a rare book librarian. The journals listed below will help you stay on top of the latest research. You should also view these journals as possible venues for your own research.

- *Book History*. University Park, PA: Pennsylvania State University Press, 1998–. An annual published by Society for the History of Authorship, Reading and Publishing (SHARP).
- *Journal of the Early Book Society for the Study of Manuscripts and Printing History*. New York: Pace University Press, 1997–.
- *The Library*. Oxford University Press [etc.] 1899–.
- *The Papers of the Bibliographical Society of America*. Chicago: University of Chicago Press, 1913–.
- *Publishing History*. Cambridge, England; Teaneck, NJ: Chadwyck-Healey, 1977–.
- *RBM: A Journal of Rare Books, Manuscripts, and Cultural Heritage*. Chicago: Association of College and Research Libraries, 2000–.
- *Studies in Bibliography: Papers of the Bibliographical Society of the University of Virginia*. Charlottesville, Va. The Society, 1949–.

Discussion Lists

Online discussion lists are the sites of continuing conversations regarding the study of rare books. They are also places where you can ask questions and share appropriate information. Those on the job market may also keep an eye out for job postings. Here are two lists to which rare book librarians may wish to subscribe.

- EXLIBRIS-L. A high-traffic discussion list with contributions from a range of professionals working with rare books, including librarians, professors, and book dealers. You can subscribe or view the web archives at: http://www.lsoft.com/scripts/wl.exe?SL1=EXLIBRIS-L&H=LISTSERV.INDIANA.EDU.
- Sharp-L. The discussion list for the Society for the History of Authorship, Reading and Publishing (SHARP), though you don't have to be a member to subscribe. http://www.sharpweb.org/en/discussion/sharp-l.html.

THE IMPORTANCE OF CONTINUING EDUCATION

The resources above are a sampling of the opportunities for continuing education that you will find once you are active in the field as a student or practitioner. The key word here is "active." The best thing you can do to expand your own knowledge and skills is to stay active in the field. The more people you meet, the more conferences you attend, the more projects you participate in, the more lectures you attend—the more you will grow as a rare book librarian. There is much to learn. Take joy and pride in learning it.

Ultimately that is the underlying message of this book. Contrary to popular belief, librarianship is not a shy, passive profession. Librarianship has grown into one of the most dynamic and intellectual modern professions. This is due in part to the Internet revolution and the subsequent explosion of information. Part of the Internet revolution has been a renewed interest in media and in how we receive and circulate information. Thus, there is a renewed interest in books, both in terms of the history of the book and the future of the book. Rare book librarians are a key part of both conversations. In this way, the rare book librarians get the best of both worlds. We need to rise to the challenge.

FINAL MESSAGE

This book began with a discussion of the idea that for special collections it is "our time." We believe this to be true. Whether working in a library, archive, or museum, it is undoubtedly an exciting time to be in the cultural heritage field. But each person who enters the field must work hard to make it "our time." We all must strive to acquire, conserve, describe, and create access to our materials both in-house and online. It is a challenging responsibility, but an enjoyable and fulfilling one. We wish you the best of luck.

CHAPTER 12

Selected Reference Resources

From guides that will help you describe books, to resources that will help you assess a book's current momentary value, there is an abundance of reference resources available both in print and online to aid rare book librarians. Below is a selected list of some of the major resources, but they are only the tip of the iceberg.

The list begins with two reference resources that every rare book librarian needs on his or her bookshelf: Gaskell's *New Introduction to Bibliography* and Carter and Barker's *ABC for Book Collectors*. Read Gaskell to learn descriptive bibliography and how books were made in both the hand-press and machine-press eras. Once you're finished with Gaskell, memorize all the terms in the *ABC*. With a working knowledge of these books, you should hit the ground running.

Gaskell, Philip. *A New Introduction to Bibliography*. New Castle, DE, and Winchester: Oak Knoll Press and St. Paul's Bibliographies, 2009.

Carter, John, and Nicolas Barker. *ABC for Book Collectors*. New Castle, DE: Oak Knoll Press; London: British Library, 2004. Available online at: www.ilab.org/download.php?object=documentation&id=29.

THE BIBLIOGRAPHY ON BIBLIOGRAPHY TO END ALL BIBLIOGRAPHIES

Tanselle, G. Thomas. *Introduction to Bibliography: Seminar Syllabus*. Charlottesville: Book Arts Press, University of Virginia, 2002. Available online: http://www.rarebookschool.org/tanselle/.

This comprehensive bibliography is a magisterial compilation of resources related to bibliography and the history of the book. The only caveat is the last update was in 2002.

BIBLIOGRAPHY AND BOOK TERMINOLOGY

Antiquarian Booksellers Association of American, Glossary of Common Trade Terms, http://hq.abaa.org/books/antiquarian/glossaryall.

Bowers, Fredson. *Principles of Bibliographical Description*. Winchester and New Castle, Delaware: St Paul's Bibliographies and Oak Knoll Press, 2005.
    Until Gaskell, Bowers's *Principles* was the standard for learning how to describe books as material objects.

Glaister, Geoffrey Ashall. *Encyclopedia of the Book*. New Castle, DE: Oak Knoll Press, 1996.

A Manual of European Languages for Librarians. London: Bowker-Saur, 1999.

McKenzie, D. F. *Bibliography and the Sociology of Texts: The Panizzi Lectures 1985* (London: The British Library, 1986).
    In order to truly understand modern bibliography and the field of the History of the Book, you must read the work of D. F. McKenzie. His essay "Bibliography and the Sociology of Texts" is a perfect place to start.

McKerrow, Ronald B., with introduction by David McKitterick. *An Introduction to Bibliography for Literary Students*. Oxford: Oxford University Press, 1927; rpt. Winchester and New Castle, DE: St. Paul's Bibliographies and Oak Knoll Press, 1994.

Moxon, Joseph. *Mechanick Exercises on the Whole Art of Printing (1683–84) by*. Edited by Herbert Davis and Harry Carter. New York: Dover Publications, 1978, 1962.

RBMS Bibliographic Standards Committee. *Latin Place Names Found in the Imprints of Books Printed BEFORE 1801 and Their Vernacular Equivalents in AACR2 (Anglo-American Cataloguing Rules) Form*, http://net.lib.byu.edu/~catalog/people/rlm/latin/names.htm.
    The imprints found on early books printed in Latin will often provided a Latinized name of the place of publication. This guide provides Latin place names and their vernacular equivalent.

RBMS Controlled Vocabularies: Controlled Vocabularies for Use in Rare Book and Special Collections Cataloging, http://www.rbms.info/committees/bibliographic_standards/controlled_vocabularies/index.shtml.
    Produced by the Bibliographic Standards Committee of the Rare Books and Manuscripts Section (ACRL/ALA), "these thesauri provide

standardized vocabulary for retrieving special collections materials by form, genre, or by various physical characteristics that are typically of interest to researchers and special collections librarians, and for relating materials to individuals or corporate bodies."

Roberts, Matt T., and Don Etherington. *Bookbinding and the Conservation of Books: A Dictionary of Descriptive Terminology*, http://cool .conservation-us.org/don//.

Librarians and curators share a basic vocabulary with book conservators, but there are many additional terms used by conservators to describe books and conservation treatments. This dictionary will help you stay on the same page as the conservators with whom you work.

BOOK HISTORY

Pearson, David. *Books as History*. London: British Library; New Castle, DE: Oak Knoll Press, 2008.

Pearson, David. *Provenance Research in Book History: A Handbook*. London: British Library; New Castle, DE: Oak Knoll Press, 1998 printing.

BOOK ILLUSTRATION

Gascoigne, Bamber. *How to Identify Prints: A Complete Guide to Manual and Mechanical Processes from Woodcut to Inkjet*, 2nd ed. New York: Thames and Hudson, 2004.

Harthan, John. *The History of the Illustrated Book: The Western Tradition*. London: Thames and Hudson, 1997.

BOOKBINDING

Greenfield, Jane. *ABC of Bookbinding: A Unique Glossary with over 700 Illustrations for Collectors and Librarians*. New Castle, DE: Oak Knoll Press; New York: Lyons Press, 1998.

Middleton, Bernard C. *A History of English Craft Bookbinding Technique*, 4th rev. ed. London: British Library; New Castle, DE: Oak Knoll Press, 1996.

Pearson, David. *English Bookbinding Styles: 1450–1800*. New Castle, DE: Oak Knoll Books, 2005.

CATALOGS AND FULL-TEXT RESOURCES, SELECTED

Bibliothèque nationale (France). *Catalogue général des livres imprimés de la Bibliothèque nationale. Auteurs*. Paris: Impr. nationale, 1897–1981.

Blanck, Jacob, ed. (later volumes edited by Michael Winship), *Bibliography of American Literature*. New Haven: Yale University Press, 1955–1991, *Epitome* and *Selective Index*, 1995.

Early European Books (EEB), http://eeb.chadwyck.co.uk/.
A subscription database providing digital facsimiles of approximately 2,600 Continental books printed prior to 1710.

English Short Title Catalogue, http://estc.bl.uk/
The ESTC, as it is more commonly called, is a free, online catalog listing over 460,000 items published in the British Isles and North America or in the English language between 1473 and 1800. Catalog records provide bibliographic information and also list the institutions that own copies. This can be helpful in determining the rarity of a book in your collection or for locating additional copies for your users to consult.

Evans, Charles. *American Bibliography; A Chronological Dictionary OF All Books, Pamphlets, AND Periodical Publications Printed in the United States of America from the Genesis of Printing in 1639 down to and Including the Year 1820*. New York: P. Smith, 1941–1967.

> Bristol, Roger P., and Charles Evans. *Index of Printers, Publishers, and Booksellers Indicated by Charles Evans in his American Bibliography*. Charlottesville: Bibliographical Society of the University of Virginia, 1961.
> Shoemaker, Richard H. *A Checklist of American Imprints for 1820–1829*. New York: Scarecrow Press, 1964–1971.
> Shoemaker, Richard H. *A Checklist of American Imprints for 1830–1839*. Metuchen, NJ: Scarecrow Press, 1972–1988.

The Incunabula Short-Title Catalogue (ISTC), http://www.bl.uk/catalogues/istc/index.html.
A catalog of incunabula (books printed prior to 1501) held at the British Library and at contributing institutions such as the Bayerische Staatsbibliothek, Munich; the Biblioteca Nazionale Centrale, Rome; and the Bibliographical Society of America.

A Short-Title Catalogue of Books Printed in England, Scotland, and Ireland and of English Books Printed Abroad, 1475–1640, ed. A. W. Pollard and G. R. Redgrave. 2nd ed. rev. and enl. / begun by W. A. Jackson and F. S. Ferguson, completed by Katharine F. Pantzer. London: Bibliographical Society, 1976–1991.
Short-title Catalogue of Books Printed in England, Scotland, Ireland, Wales, and British America and of English Books Printed in Other Countries, 1641–1700, ed. Donald Wing. 2nd ed., revised and edited by John J. Morrison and Carolyn W. Nelson, editors, and Matthew Seccombe,

assistant editor. New York: Modern Language Association of America, 1994–1998.

Tanselle, G. Thomas. *Guide to the Study of United States Imprints*. Cambridge: Belknap Press of Harvard University Press, 1971.

The Universal Short Title Catalogue (USTC), http://www.ustc.ac.uk/.

The USTC "is a project aimed at bringing together information on all books published in Europe between the invention of printing and the end of the sixteenth century." As most catalogs tend to be geographically defined, the USTC holds great promise as a comprehensive tool for librarians and book historians that will spark interdisciplinary work.

CONSERVATION AND PRESERVATION

Appelbaum, Barbara. *Conservation Treatment Methodology*. Amsterdam; Boston: Butterworth-Heinemann, 2007.

Balloffet, Nelly, and Jenny Hille. *Preservation and Conservation for Libraries and Archives*. Chicago: American Library Association, 2005.

Greenfield, Jane. *The Care of Fine Books*. New York: Skyhorse Publishing, 2007.

Ogden, Sherelyn, ed. *Preservation of Library and Archival Materials: A Manual*, 3rd ed. Andover, MA: Northeast Document Conservation Center (NEDCC), 1999.

HISTORY OF RARE BOOK LIBRARIES

Feather, John P., and David McKitterick. *The History of Books and Libraries: Two Views*. Washington, DC: Library of Congress, 1986.

Johnson, Elmer D. *History of Libraries in the Western World*. New York: Scarecrow Press, 1965; rpt. Metuchen, NJ: Scarecrow Press, 1995, 4th ed., rev. by Michael H. Harris.

Joyce, William L. "The Evolution of the Concept of Special Collections in American Research Libraries." *Rare Books & Manuscripts Librarianship* 3 (1988): 19–29.

Rare Book Collections: Some Theoretical and Practical Suggestions for Use by Librarians and Students, ed. H. Richard Archer. Chicago: American Library Association, 1965.

Under the Hammer: Book Auctions since the Seventeenth Century, ed. Robin Myers, Michael Harris, and Giles Mandelbrote. New Castle, DE: Oak Knoll Press; London: The British Library, 2001.

MANUSCRIPTS AND EARLY BOOKS

De Hamel, Christopher. *A History of Illuminated Manuscripts*. Oxford: Phaidon, 1986, rpt. 1994.

Ricci, Seymour de, and W. J. Wilson. *Census of Medieval and Renaissance Manuscripts in the United States and Canada*, 3 vols. New York: H. W. Wilson, 1935–1940. Supplement. Originated by C. U. Faye, continued and edited by W. H. Bond. New York: Bibliographical Society of America, 1962.

MODERN PRINTING

Anderson, Patricia. *The Printed Image and the Transformation of Popular Culture, 1790–1860*. Oxford, UK: Clarendon Press; New York: Oxford University Press, 1991.

Brodhead, Richard H. *Cultures of Letters: Scenes of Reading and Writing in Nineteenth-Century America*. Chicago: University of Chicago Press, 1993.

Denning, Michael. *Mechanic Accents: Dime Novels and Working-Class Culture in America*. London; New York: Verso, 1987.

Lee, Alan J. *The Origins of the Popular Press in England, 1855–1914*. London: Croom Helm; Totowa, NJ: Rowman and Littlefield, 1976.

McDonald, Peter D. *British Literary Culture and Publishing Practice, 1880–1914*. Cambridge, UK; New York: Cambridge University Press, 1997.

Morrisson, Mark. *The Public Face of Modernism: Little Magazines, Audiences, and Reception, 1905–1920*. Madison: University of Wisconsin Press, 2001.

Radway, Janice A. *A Feeling for Books: The Book-of-the-Month Club, Literary Taste, and Middle-Class Desire*. Chapel Hill: University of North Carolina Press, 1997.

Rubin, Joan Shelley. *The Making of Middlebrow Culture*. Chapel Hill: University of North Carolina Press, 1992.

Weedon, Alexis. *Victorian Publishing: The Economics of Book Production for a Mass Market, 1830–1916*. Aldershot, UK; Burlington, VT: Ashgate, 2002.

Wicke, Jennifer. *Advertising Fictions: Literature, Advertisement and Social Reading*. New York: Columbia University Press, 1988.

PEOPLE

American National Biography, http://www.anb.org. This subscription database "offers portraits of more than 18,700 men and women—from all eras and walks of life—whose lives have shaped the nation."

Oxford Dictionary of National Biography, http://www.oxforddnb.com/. This subscription database provides biographies for "the men and women from around the world who shaped all aspects of Britain's past."

PRINTING AND PUBLISHING HISTORY

Blagden, Cyprian. *The Stationers' Company: A History, 1403–1959*. Cambridge: Harvard University Press, 1960, rpt. Stanford: Stanford University Press, 1977.

The Cambridge History of the Book in Britain, 6 vols. Cambridge, UK; New York: Cambridge University Press, 1999–.

Eisenstein, Elizabeth. *The Printing Press as an Agent of Change: Communications and Cultural Transformations in Early Modern Europe*, 2 vols. Cambridge, UK: Cambridge University Press, 1979; rpt. paperback edition, 2 vols. in one, 1980.

A History of the Book in America Volume, 5 vols. Chapel Hill, N.C.: Published in association with the American Antiquarian Society by the University of North Carolina Press, 1999–2010.

Incunabula and Their Readers: Printing, Selling and Using Books in the Fifteenth Century. Edited by Kristian Jensen. London: British Library, 2003.

Johns, Adrian. *The Nature of the Book: Print and Knowledge in the Making* (1998). Chicago: University of Chicago Press, 1998.

Lehmann-Haupt, Hellmut, Lawrence Wroth, and Ruth S. Granniss. *The Book in America: A History of the Making and Selling of Books in the United States*. New York: R. R. Bowker, 1939. 2nd revised and enlarged edition (with Rollo G. Silver replacing Granniss), 1952.

McKitterick, David. *Print, Manuscript and the Search for Order, 1450–1830*. Cambridge and New York: Cambridge University Press, 2003.

Mumby, Frank A. *Publishing and Bookselling: A History from the Earliest Times to the Present Day*. London: J. Cape, 1930. 5th Edition, revised and reset by Ian Norrie. London: J. Cape, 1974.

Myers, Robin. *The Stationers' Company: A History of the Later Years, 1800–2000*. Chichester, UK: Published for the Worshipful Co. of Stationers & Newspaper Makers by Phillimore, 2001.

Pettegree, Andrew. *The Book in the Renaissance*. New Haven, CT: Yale University Press, 2010.

Twyman, Michael. *The British Library Guide to Printing History and Techniques*. Toronto: University of Toronto Press, 1998.

PROVENANCE AND APPRAISAL RESOURCES

Auction Houses, Searching Auction Results

Bloomsbury Auctions: http://www.bloomsburyauctions.com/ (see search box in the lower left-hand corner of the page)

Bonhams: http://www.bonhams.com/auctions/ (choose the "Past" tab and search)

Christie's: http://www.christies.com/LotFinder/advanced_search.aspx.

Sotheby's: http://www.sothebys.com (under "Auctions" choose "Sold Lot Archive").

Reference Resources

American Book Prices Current. New York: Bancroft-Parkman, 1894–.

Records the prices of books and other artifacts sold at auction in North America and the UK, as well as various auction houses through Europe. Also available as an online subscription database: http://www.bookpricescurrent .com/Online.aspx.

Bookman's Price Index. Detroit: Gale Research, 1964–.

Records the prices of books offered in the catalogs of book dealers in the United States, Canada, and the British Isles.

INDEX

Page numbers followed by f indicate figure

About the Authors

STEVEN K. GALBRAITH is Curator of the Cary Graphic Arts Collection at Rochester Institute of Technology. He has a Ph.D. in English Literature from The Ohio State University and an M.L.S. from the University at Buffalo. Prior to coming to RIT, he was the Andrew W. Mellon Curator of Books at the Folger Shakespeare Library in Washington, DC, the Curator of Early Modern Books and Manuscripts at The Ohio State University, and a reference librarian at the University of Maine. He is the author of *The Undergraduate's Companion to English Renaissance Writers and Their Web Sites* and has served as general editor of the Undergraduate's Companion Series and the Author Research Series for Libraries Unlimited. He has written articles and reports on early English printing, book conservation and digitization, and the poet Edmund Spenser.

GEOFFREY D. SMITH is the Head of the Rare Books and Manuscripts Library at The Ohio State University. He holds a PhD in American Literature and Textual Studies from Indiana University. He is the author of *American Fiction, 1901–1925: A Bibliography* (1997), and is general editor for a series of textual editions of William S. Burroughs under The Ohio State University Press. The first volume of the Burroughs series, *Everything Lost: The Latin American Notebooks of William S. Burroughs*, was published in December 2007. He has written critical articles on Henry James, Nathaniel Hawthorne, and William Dean Howells, in addition to numerous publications on rare book and textual studies topics.